Linking Education Policy to
Labor Market Outcomes

Linking Education Policy to Labor Market Outcomes

Tazeen Fasih

 THE WORLD BANK

Cover photo: World Bank Photo Library
DOI:10.1596/978-0-8213-7509-9

Library of Congress Cataloging-in-Publication Data

Fasih, Tazeen, 1972-
Linking education policy to labor market outcomes / Tazeen Fasih.
p. cm.
Includes bibliographical references and index.
ISBN-13: 978-0-8213-7509-9 (alk. paper)
ISBN-10: 0-8213-7509-1 (alk. paper)
ISBN-13: 978-0-8213-7510-5 (e-bk)
1. Labor supply--Developing countries--Education. 2. Economic development--Effect of education on. 3. Education--Developing countries. I. Title.
HD5852.F376 2008
331.11'423091724--dc22
2008008390

Contents

Figures

Tables

Boxes

Preface

Education plays a central role in preparing individuals to enter the labor force, as well as equipping them with the skills to engage in lifelong learning experiences. There are, however, numerous dimensions of education–labor market linkages. Rapid expansion of education has not necessarily been accompanied by rapid economic growth in many developing countries. The education and labor market work program of the World Bank has emerged out of a need to (i) conceptualize a holistic education–labor market framework, (ii) identify the key policy issues faced both by World Bank education task teams and client country policy makers, and (iii) provide policy advice on how countries can use their education systems to contribute to the rapid growth of their respective economies and explain why other countries have failed to do so.

The first phase of the work program focuses on the conceptual framework for studying the linkage between education markets and labor markets and seeks to identify the key policy issues that need to be addressed for education to contribute to positive labor market outcomes. The second phase of the work program will focus on evidence from a wide range of countries to identify who benefits most from education, and the final phase will identify concrete policy actions that have benefited countries in the development of an educated, skilled workforce that has helped these countries grow in the global economy.

Acknowledgments

This report was prepared by Tazeen Fasih (Task Team Leader). Alonso Sanchez provided valuable research assistance during its preparation. Significant contributions were made by Geeta Kingdon, Marco Manacorda, Mans Soderbom, Francis Teal, and Jesus Lopez-Macedo. The report greatly benefited from the comments of Harry Patrinos, Felipe Barrera, Veronica Grigera, and of peer reviewers Amit Dar and Michel Welmond. The inputs of Vicente Moreno-Garcia and Seemeen Saadat at different stages of the report preparation are gratefully acknowledged. Peggy McInerny provided excellent editing of the content. The report was prepared under the overall guidance of Ruth Kagia and Robin Horn. The two country case studies were prepared with support from the country teams, including Setareh Razmarah, Tahseen Sayed, S. Ramachandran, and Michel Welmond. The report was funded by a World Bank–Netherlands Partnership Program.

Overview

The objective of this study is to review what is known about the role of education in improving labor market outcomes, with a particular focus on policy considerations for developing countries. The report presents findings from current literature on the topic, which offer new ways of looking at the returns to education, together with evidence from four original data analysis and background studies of education and labor issues in Ghana and Pakistan.

Country studies on Ghana and Pakistan are used to substantiate findings of the literature and illustrate the heterogeneity of education–labor market linkages across regions. These countries were chosen because they are representative of two of the poorest regions of the world and because their inclusion in the analysis complements ongoing World Bank work on education and labor market issues in those countries.

Key Findings

This report offers two types of findings: those relevant to the content of educational policies and those relevant to the framework for educational policy making. Specifically, the report argues that educational policies need to be seen within a broader macroeconomic context if education is to contribute to national economic growth. For example, policies aimed at improving the skills of the workforce will have limited impact on the incomes of those who acquire the skills, or on the performance of a national economy, unless both labor and nonlabor policies are in place that increase the demand for these skills.

Educational Policy Content

Education continues to yield high returns to individuals. Basic literacy and numeracy generate excellent returns in labor markets in developing economies, although the scale of these returns depends on the country context and the country's level of economic development.

If, however, the attainment of these basic skills takes 8 to 12 years of education, as in the systems in the countries analyzed in this report, the system is extremely inefficient. Similarly, if a 15-year-old enrolled in school is unable to use his or her literacy skills for further learning and attainment of knowledge, as indicated by low proficiency scores in international student assessments, the education system has failed the individual.

The Millennium Development Goals assume that the completion of primary education, along with the achievement of the other goals, will help realize the goal of cutting in half the number of people living in poverty worldwide by 2015. **The data analyzed in this report indicate that just increasing the quantity of education at the lower educational levels will not raise earnings substantially, and thus not prove to be effective in helping people climb out of poverty.** Given the increasing demand for skills and the development of skills-biased technology, it could be that the returns to primary education are low. However, the returns could also be low because educational systems are failing to produce minimum functional literacy and numeracy skills at the primary level. In either case, the provision of high-quality, subsidized primary education continues to be warranted, not only because it empowers people and helps reduce inequality, but because countries with low levels of education could otherwise remain trapped in technological stagnation and low growth.

In spite of improved primary education completion rates, fewer individuals might be attaining competitive skill sets. The *World Development Report 2007* (World Bank 2006) suggests that although curricula and teaching methods have remained largely unchanged in developing countries over the years, employers are increasingly demanding strong thinking, communication, and entrepreneurial skills—demands largely unmet by educational systems in the developing and transition economies. Both general and core competencies and skills have become increasingly valuable in labor markets that are characterized by change and in which there is a constant need to adapt to new developments in technology and working methods.

The literature on human capital accumulation indicates that high-quality education at the primary level generates the highest returns, both at the primary level and all levels thereafter. Early investment in cognitive and noncognitive skills produces a high return and lowers the cost of later educational investment by making learning at later ages more efficient. When investments are made in individuals at a later stage in their lives, in adolescence, for example, or when the quality of skills provided at the earlier stage of education is low, then baseline skills and the marginal productivity of later educational investments will also be low. Therefore, investing in quality learning in early childhood is essential. Recent evidence suggests that the earlier in childhood these investments are made to develop cognitive and social skills, the better the long-term impacts on skills and labor market outcomes. Evidence also suggests that the efficiency of education at this level would be further enhanced by parallel investments in children's health.

Improvements to the quality and efficiency of basic education are urgently needed, in both developing and transition countries. These goals require policies that focus on (i) improving the efficiency of educational spending, so that the development of core skills does not require eight or more years, and (ii) adapting the curriculum of basic as well as postbasic education to develop the skills increasingly in demand in the global labor market: critical thinking, problem solving, and behavioral (that is, noncognitive) skills, as well as skills in information technology.

Although a number of studies indicate that achieving literacy and numeracy skills in developing countries has a high cost, more research on this topic is needed. In fact, the direct and indirect costs of developing these basic skills are not commonly estimated in the literature. By the standards defined by UNESCO, such basic skills should be completely mastered by the end of the primary school cycle, that is, with five years of schooling; however, evidence suggesting the need for 8–12 years of schooling to attain these skills points to the high cost of the attainment of these skills.

Multisectoral Framework for Educational Policy

Different macroeconomic and country contexts create very different labor market demands and associated rewards, suggesting that educational policy needs do not follow traditional development groupings or categories. Given the heterogeneity of labor market outcomes for individuals with the same level of education, not all individuals benefit equally from education in the labor market of a given country, nor do all levels of education reap similar rewards. With respect to Ghana and Pakistan, it is revealing that these developing countries show different patterns in returns to education. In Pakistan, high returns are seen at all levels of education, particularly among women in wage employment, and these increase at higher levels of education, whereas higher returns are apparent only at the highest level of education in Ghana.

To gain a comprehensive picture of education–labor market linkages in any country, supply-side analysis needs to be complemented with demand-side analysis. If education is to promote economic growth, educational policies must consider both the supply of education (quality and efficiency) and the demand for education (labor market policy, specifically, and nonlabor policies that affect the labor market, such as foreign direct investment [FDI] and technological development). Without an integrated, multisectoral approach to educational policy, the links between nonlabor policies and the labor market can result in a mismatch between education and the skills in demand.

The role that FDI flows, trade penetration, and industrial policies play in inducing skills-biased technological change, and thus affecting the demand for education, merits greater research. In particular, the issues of how demand for education increases with broader policy changes in the global economy and how countries can ensure that they maintain a competitive workforce (capable of responding to the changing needs of the economy) need to be better understood.

Policies aimed at improving the skills of the workforce will have limited impact on the incomes of those who acquire these skills, or on the performance of a national economy, unless other policies are in place that increase the demand for those skills. In Ghana, for example, the largest demand for labor is overwhelmingly in the domestic market, where self-employment has expanded much more rapidly than wage employment. The return to skills in the domestic market is, however, very low. These two facts are linked. As long as the demand for low-educated labor fails to rise as fast as the supply, the price of skills will inevitably remain low.

While improving the quality and quantity of skills is part of any educational package, it is only part—the package will fail unless the issue of job creation is addressed. The supply of adequate jobs for the labor force is a central concern of any policy maker. However, the issue is not simply whether an adequate number of jobs exist, but whether these jobs are of adequate quality.

If the major issues that affect education–labor market linkages originate in the demand side of the labor market, further expansion of education is unwarranted without attempting to address these issues. For example, subsidies in tertiary education need to be accompanied by the creation of an environment conducive to investment and technological progress. In the absence of such an environment, countries will find their population emigrating for better opportunities and governments will need to continue subsidizing education to compensate for weak effective demand.

The framework within which educational supply and demand are analyzed needs to be broadened to include a country's macroeconomic situation, investment climate, and labor market policies. A more comprehensive framework will not only strengthen the diagnostic capacity of education supply and demand analysis, it will also streamline the policy approach to education issues.

CHAPTER 1

Introduction

Recent years have seen renewed interest in the study of the links between education and labor market success, motivated by a search for the causes of growing disparities between more- and less-educated workers and by the existing wage differentials for workers with the same level of education. Concurrently, policy concerns have arisen about the relative costs and benefits of various levels of education, in particular, postbasic and higher education in countries worldwide. A new focus on the roles of both quantity and quality of human capital in the development process, moreover, has given policy makers new appreciation of the importance of education–labor market linkages.

The objective of this study is to review what is known about the role of education in improving labor market outcomes, with a particular focus on policy considerations for developing countries. The report presents findings from current literature on the topic, which offer new ways of looking at the returns to education, together with evidence from four original data analysis and background studies of education and labor issues in Ghana and Pakistan.

The Ghana and Pakistan country studies are used to substantiate findings of the literature and illustrate the heterogeneity of education–labor market linkages across regions. These countries were chosen because they are representative of two of the poorest regions of the world and because their inclusion in the analysis complements ongoing World Bank work on education and labor market issues in those countries.

The standard human capital model is based on the idea that individuals choose their optimal level of education so as to equalize marginal returns and marginal costs (Becker 1964). Although estimating such returns requires complex econometric analysis of education–labor market linkages, this type of analysis remains the most commonly used method for determining how individuals benefit from education and for estimating the poverty-reducing potential of different levels of education.

For a comprehensive picture of education–labor market linkages, however, this supply-side analysis needs to be complemented with demand-side analysis. The supply of adequate jobs for the labor force is a central concern of any policy maker. However, the issue is not simply an adequate number of jobs for the workforce, but whether these jobs are of adequate quality. The two groups of issues that need to be explored from the demand side, therefore, include policy issues related to markets other than labor markets and policy issues that affect the operation of labor markets. The former might include government policy on foreign direct investment (FDI) or technological advancement (de Ferranti et al. 2003), whereas the latter might more directly concern labor market regulations and the match (or mismatch) of skills and education in labor markets.

Education and relevant skills remain the main determinants of good labor market outcomes for individuals. Although labor market outcomes depend on a myriad of factors—household labor supply decisions, the influence of the product market on the labor market, the investment climate in a given country, growth and productivity, financial markets, and FDI—**education and skills can be regarded as necessary, but by no means sufficient, for achieving favorable labor market outcomes.** A country's development and edge in the global economy, therefore, depend on the creation of a highly skilled workforce with the ability to access, adapt, apply, and create new knowledge and technologies.

Education plays a central role in preparing individuals to enter the labor force and in equipping them with the skills needed to engage in lifelong learning experiences. Vast research literature provides evidence of the value of investing in education to develop human capital and of its contribution to economic development and growth (see, for example, Hanushek and Kimko 2000; Krueger and Lindahl 2000; Hanushek and Woessmann 2007). The primacy of education stems not only from its fundamental role in increasing individual earnings, but also from its *noneconomic* benefits—such as lower infant mortality, better participation in democracy, reduced crime, and even the simple the joy of learning—that enhance and enrich the quality of life and sustain development (Case 2001). Economists have speculated that these social returns to education may be higher even than the private returns, where returns are defined simply as the benefits of education net of its costs (Currie and Moretti 2003; Moretti 2004a, 2004b).

Economic policy interest in education is, in general, linked to its potential to increase earnings and reduce poverty. Much of the focus in the literature has thus been on *economic* returns to education. Estimates of the returns to different levels of education (primary, secondary, tertiary), different types of education (general and vocational), and different subjects (medicine, law, agriculture, humanities, and so on) are extensively used for various policy and evaluation purposes. For instance, intrasectoral budgetary allocations are sometimes justified on the basis of the estimated returns to different levels and types of education. Similarly, some governments consider the economic returns to different degree subjects in setting fees for different university courses.

This report emphasizes the importance of a holistic approach to analyzing education–labor market issues, with particular stress on education market diagnosis. **The role of education needs to be seen in a broader macroeconomic context to ensure that education contributes to the growth of a country's economy.** The role of FDI flows, trade penetration, and industrial policies in inducing skills-biased technological change, and the impact that these factors have on the demand for education, is an under-researched area of inquiry. Specifically, this study calls for a focus on how demand for education increases with broader policy changes in the global economy and how countries can ensure that they maintain competitive workforces (ones capable of responding to the changing needs of the economy).

Written from the perspective of an education specialist, **this study attempts to identify the key policy issues that facilitate education's role in improving labor market outcomes, through both better access to opportunities and better returns to education.** Micro data from the Ghana and Pakistan country studies are used throughout the report to illustrate the complexities of education–labor market linkages.[1] Chapter 2 develops the conceptual framework for understanding education–labor market linkages. Based on this framework, chapter 3 assesses the supply of education measured by educational outcomes and their impacts on labor market outcomes. Chapter 4 discusses the demand for labor within the broader policy context and draws mainly on the Ghana case study. Chapter 5 concludes with the major policy implications revealed by the analysis. The appendixes present supplemental information on both methodology and educational research. Appendix 1 presents a brief summary of the method commonly used to analyze education–labor market linkages; appendix 2, the methodology used for the Pakistan and Ghana case studies; and appendix 3 summarizes a number of studies on returns to basic educational skills conducted in countries worldwide.

Note

1. In addition to household surveys, the Ghana studies also make use of existing data and analysis from the Ghana Manufacturing and Enterprise Survey (similar to the Investment Climate Assessment Survey of the World Bank) to explore demand aspects of the Ghanaian labor markets.

CHAPTER 2

The Conceptual Framework

At the most basic level, the linkages between education and the labor market can be defined as a three-tiered relationship: the determinants of education determine educational outcomes, which, in turn, determine the labor market outcomes of individuals (see figure 2.1). The relationship between the education "market" and labor markets is, however, much more intricate, with many players active at various levels. Most important, the country context (seen at the extreme right-hand side of figure 2.1) plays an overarching role in the school-to-work transition and education decisions made at the micro level. This context includes welfare systems (for example, free education, incentives for education at different levels, the social protection system, and labor market support to the unemployed), as well as the overall macroeconomic context.

The first tier of linkages—the determinants of education—include demand-side as well as supply-side factors (seen as the first horizontal row in figure 2.1). **On the demand side, these determinants are child and family characteristics and community and societal characteristics. On the supply side, they are school characteristics and other inputs.** Governments can and do influence how these four determinants affect educational outcomes. For instance, schools in most developing countries are generally administered by national governments, which have considerable authority over such crucial issues as school facilities, pedagogy, language of instruction, textbooks and other materials, and the training of teachers, among many other factors.

The perceived quality of schooling that a government supplies its citizens affects the demand for that education because, if given a choice, families are more likely to enroll their children in good schools. Certain other policies also affect demand-side determinants of educational outcomes. For instance, government incentives, such as targeted reductions of school fees or conditional cash transfers, have proved successful in encouraging families to send their children to school in numerous countries.

At the second tier of educational outcomes, the quality and quantity of education are determined by a range of factors, including an individual's family and community, school characteristics, time spent in the education system, and the type of education.[1] Number of years spent in the formal education system is a first-order educational outcome. This time enables students to attain higher-order educational outcomes, such as skills and degrees, which often function as signals that a person possesses useful skills and knowledge. In this context, a general versus technical or vocational educational track has strong repercussions on labor market entry. **Important educational outcomes thus include cognitive and technical skills; general and specific knowledge; and values that help prepare individuals to enjoy healthy, productive, and fulfilling lives.** Degrees attained and grades completed, however, often remain among the key determinants of labor market outcomes because people who have an adequate education have more chances of ending up employed.

Labor markets, broadly defined as the buying and selling of labor services (Fields 2007), are distinguished by two types of employment: (i) wage and salaried employment, where labor is sold to others; and (ii) self-employment, where workers sell services and labor to themselves. Although an oversimplification, because the definitions of formal and informal employment encompass a number of other dimensions, wage and salaried employment largely falls under formal employment and self-employment falls under informal employment.

As seen in figure 2.1, **employment is the basic labor market outcome of education for individuals.** There are three fundamental ways in which education affects this outcome. First, those with fewer skills, less knowledge, and fewer degrees are less attractive to potential employers and less prepared to start their own businesses. Second, individuals who followed

Figure 2.1   Basic framework of education--labor market linkages

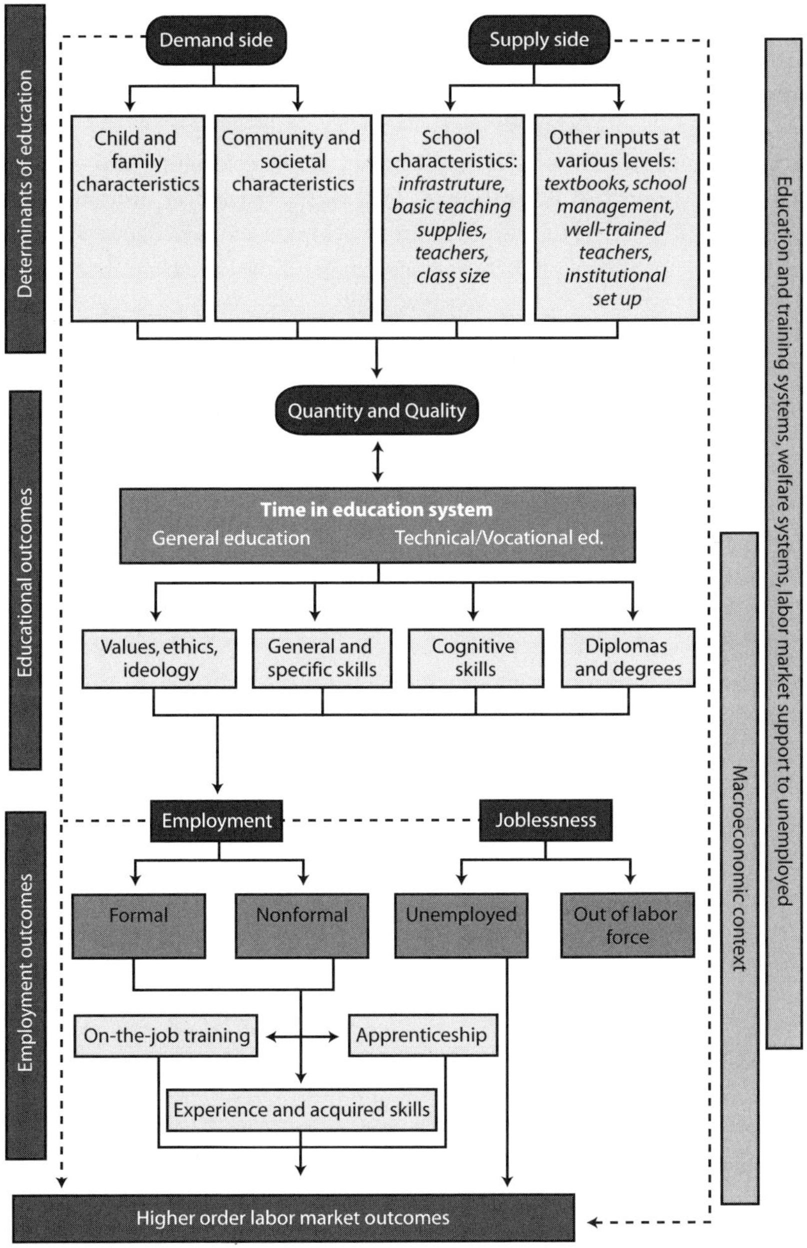

Source: Author.

a vocational or technical education track will enter different occupations from those who followed a general education track. In fact, most labor market models with skill differentials are based on this assumption. A third way in which educational attainment affects employment is by ensuring greater earnings within an occupation (although much depends on the quality of education as well).

In both formal and informal employment, apprenticeships and on-the-job training are part of education as well as labor market outcomes. In particular, formal schooling systems in developing economies, especially those with large, pervasive informal sectors, may not be the only important channel for acquiring employment skills. Many workers acquire skills through apprenticeships in informal or traditional training systems. While often directly linked to the labor market, the skills that such apprentices acquire may or may not enable them to access higher-skill and better-remunerated employment opportunities. In certain cases, but more likely in formal than in informal employment sectors, governments can establish policies that encourage firms and small businesses to offer apprentice or training activities or positions if these outcomes appear desirable.

The second possible initial labor market outcome is joblessness, a category that combines the unemployed (people who are not working, but available and seeking work) and those who are out of the labor force. Although unemployment may be a normal state during the job entry process, extended spells of inactivity tend to have strong associations with issues such as health problems, drug addiction, and social unrest (O'Higgins 2002), and therefore merit special attention from policy makers.

Finally, another important consideration in labor market outcomes is that employment status can change over time—people who are employed can become unemployed and vice versa throughout their working lives. This change of status is indicated in figure 2.1 by a dashed line because it does not imply causality.

Higher-order labor market outcomes are affected by educational outcomes and their determinants, as well as by previous employment. For people who are formally employed, higher-order outcomes can include increased wages and access to further on-the-job training and promotions. For people who are informally employed, these outcomes can include enhanced productivity, access to credit, and business expansion, among others. Finally, job stability and satisfaction are outcomes that accrue to both types of workers. The role that education plays in shaping outcomes at this level has been much less studied than employment outcomes, particularly in developing countries, and is thus less understood. Perhaps degrees attained by young people have greater weight during the school-to-work transition (Van der Velden 2007), whereas skills and knowledge prove more important in the long term. However, if the skills acquired in education relate to a very specific occupation, technological change could make these obsolete.

Note

1. Type of education can be the result of conscious choice or chance (that is, the type of education to which a student managed to gain access). A large number of education systems follow academic tracking, in which certain fields of education are open only to students who demonstrate high achievement in school or school exit examinations. Discussion of this topic is outside the scope of this paper and will be analyzed in an upcoming paper by Human Development Network, Education Department.

CHAPTER 3

Educational Outcomes and Their Impact on Labor Market Outcomes

Education and relevant skills are a necessary condition for good labor market outcomes for individuals. Quality, including the content of education, and quantity (number of years in education) together determine the economic impact of a particular level of education in the labor market. This chapter expands on the second tier of the framework developed in chapter 2 (see figure 2.1) by assessing the supply of education through educational outcomes and their impacts on labor market outcomes.

Basic Cognitive Skills and Quality of Education

Evidence suggests that cognitive skills have large economic effects on individual earnings and on national growth (Hanushek and Woessmann 2007) **and that workers' productivity depends both on years of education and what is learned at school** (Heckman, Layne-Farrar, and Todd 1995; Murnane, Willett, and Levy 1995). Although a number of interpretations are more encompassing, basic cognitive skills can be defined as literacy (the ability to read and write in a language) and numeracy (the ability to perform simple mathematical operations).

In the empirical literature on the effect of basic cognitive skills on earnings, both self-reported literacy and numeracy and scores on specially designed tests to measure functional literacy and numeracy from various perspectives have been used (see, for example, Boissiere, Knight, and Sabot 1985; Alderman et al. 1996; Behrman et al. 1997; Behrman, Ross, and Sabot 2002).[1] **Generally speaking, the estimated effects of basic cognitive skills on earnings are significant and positive.** One study on the United States (Murnane, Willett, and Levy 1995), for example, found that cognitive skills were strong predictors of wages during the 1980s, apparently stronger than they had been in the 1970s. Similarly, researchers found strong positive effects of numeracy and literacy on earnings in other developed countries, including Canada and the United Kingdom (McIntosh and Vignoles 2001; Finnie and Meng 2001, 2002; Green and Riddell 2003). Other research reports similar findings, including a number of studies on developing countries (see appendix 3 for a summary of several studies).[2]

Research suggests that basic literacy and numeracy skills matter greatly to people's economic outcomes, whether through the indirect effect of occupational sorting or a direct effect on earnings. In the country studies for Pakistan and Ghana, conducted to illustrate this report, wage employment and self-employment are much better remunerated occupations than agriculture. Individuals who can read and write are therefore much less likely to work in agriculture in both countries (see table 3.1).[3] Even in the informal sector, lack of basic literacy and numeracy can hinder the success of an individual in the labor market. Haan and Serriere (2002) identify these skills as one of the basic training needs in the informal sector; in its absence, trainability and consequent skill achievements are limited.

As shown in figure 3.1, the returns to being literate are high in both Pakistan and Ghana, conditional on being in one of the occupational states in table 3.1. In fact, older literate women in Pakistan earn a premium of almost 200 percent, a result that reflects the scarcity premium, because far fewer women than men are literate in the country. The picture in Ghana, where the earnings premium is not as high for women compared with men, is quite different.

Notwithstanding the high earnings premiums associated with literacy shown in figure 3.1, **an important issue for economists and policy makers is the cost associated with developing these skills in individuals,**[4] costs that are not commonly estimated in the literature. According to the

Table 3.1 Marginal effects of literacy and numeracy on occupational outcomes by gender and age group in Ghana and Pakistan
(percentage; comparative category: wage employment)

	Pakistan				Ghana	
	Young (age 30 years and younger)		Old (age > 30)		All ages (16–65)	
	Men	*Women*	*Men*	*Women*	*Men*	*Women*
1. Self-employment						
Can solve simple math problem	3.4	0.9	4.2	0.9	-0.1	10.1
Can read and write	5.2	-0.4	3.8	-0.1	1.4	1.0
2. Agriculture						
Can solve simple math problem	1.4	2.5	2.4	1.8	-9.7	-16.0
Can read and write	-9.3	-9.8	-13.6	-9.2	-18.3	-16.2
3. Unemployed						
Can solve simple math problem	1.2	-2.2	-0.7	-2.5	0.8	0.4
Can read and write	3.6	1.4	0.8	0.1	0.3	-0.1
4. Out of labor force						
Can solve simple math problem	-5.8	-3.4	-0.5	-3.2	-2.7	4.1
Can read and write	6.7	7.9	2.0	7.8	2.5	2.1

Source: Kingdon and Soderbom 2007a, 2007b.

Note: These results are based on the multinomial logits reported in the background studies on Ghana and Pakistan. See appendix 2 for a summary of the methodology. Numbers in bold are statistically significant.

International Standard Classification of Education 1997 (ISCED97), primary education—or the first five years of school—is the level at which these basic competencies should be mastered. However, a number of studies indicate that the costs associated with achieving these skills in individuals in developing countries are much higher; for instance, Hanushek and Woessmann (2007) suggest that often even nine years of schooling in an average developing country does not necessarily mean that students have become functionally literate.

Evidence for the countries evaluated for this report suggests that it takes men 10 years and women 12 years to acquire literacy in Ghana.[5] **In Pakistan, approximately 8 years of schooling are needed to acquire basic (self-reported) cognitive skills** (including the ability to read a simple sentence and write one's own name). Comparative data from the reading component of the standardized Programme for International Student Assessment (PISA), moreover, indicates that these basic cognitive skills are often insufficient to enable students to continue to advance their

Figure 3.1   Returns to basic literacy skills, Pakistan and Ghana

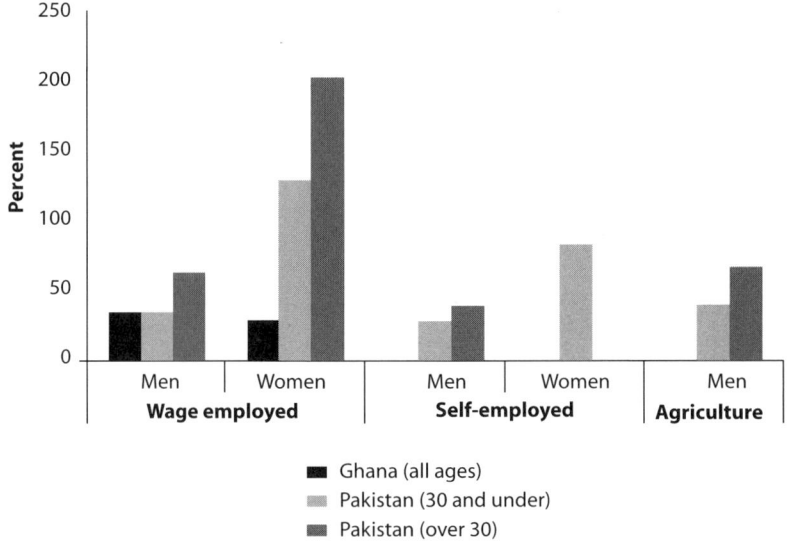

Source: Estimated from Pakistan Integrated Household Survey (PIHS) 2001–02 and Ghana Living Standards Survey (GLSS) 1998 (Kingdon and Soderbom 2007a, 2007b).

Note: Only statistically significant returns in the three employment categories are plotted.

knowledge. The Organisation for Economic Co-operation and Development's (OECD's) PISA measures the ability of individuals to construct, expand, and reflect on what they have read in a text. Low proficiency on the test (below level 1) indicates that such students have "serious difficulties in using reading literacy as an effective tool to advance and extend their knowledge and skills in other areas" (OECD 2007, p. 295). Whereas an average of 12.7 percent of students score at or below level 1 (low proficiency) on the PISA across OECD countries, more than 50 percent of students score at or below this level in a number of developing countries.[6]

These findings highlight the importance of improving the quality of schooling so that a given number of years of education lead to higher cognitive skills. A better-quality education system could produce similar literacy levels at lower cost because it would use the time and resources spent on teaching more efficiently. A study by Behrman, Ross, and Sabot (2008) suggests, for instance, that completing grade 8 in Pakistan after a low-quality primary education yields a 2.8 percent rate of return; however, a high-quality primary education would yield a return of 13.0 percent.

Recent research provides even more compelling reasons for improving the quality of education, particularly at the basic and even prebasic level. Evidence shows, for example, that there are critical, sensitive periods in the development of a child when different types of abilities appear easier to acquire (Cunha and Heckman 2007). Both cognitive and noncognitive skills build on learning attained in preceding stages of education. A similar pattern is observed in the labor market, where, according to the OECD (2007), the skill differences with which individuals leave initial education are often reinforced in job-related continuing education and training.

The literature on human capital accumulation shows that over the lifetime of an individual, early investment in cognitive and noncognitive skills produces a high return, lowering the cost of later investment by making learning at later ages more efficient. The model developed by Cunha et al. (2006), shown in figure 3.2, suggests that when educational investments are made in individuals at a later stage in life, at adolescence, for instance, the marginal productivity of such investments will be low if the quality of skills provided at earlier stages of education was low.

Returns to "Quantity" of Education: The Changing Trends

In attempting to identify the exact causal effect of education on labor market outcomes, the basic problem encountered is that innate ability and years of education are likely to be highly correlated. That is, more-able people generally find it easier to learn cognitive skills and complete higher school grades. Therefore, it is unclear whether the estimated return on education represents a return on human capital (skills acquired through education) or merely a return to ability.

Although the human capital theory suggests that education enhances worker productivity, the screening (or credentialist) hypothesis argues that employers might use education as a way to identify the most-able workers. That is, the apparent large economic returns to education might really accrue not so much to education as to ability, with which education is usually highly correlated. If true, the screening hypothesis would weaken the efficiency rationale for public investment in education, lead-

Figure 3.2   Rate of return to human capital investment

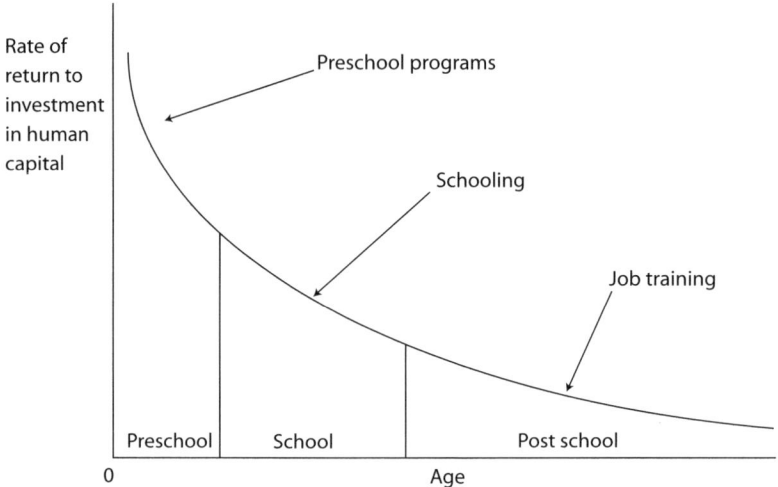

Source: Cunha et al. 2006.

ing to the conclusion that society derives less benefit from the education of individuals than do individuals themselves (that is, the social returns on education are less than the private returns).

Empirical analysis of these issues is difficult because the labor market outcomes of both the screening and the human capital models are very similar (see Hanushek and Woessmann 2007). Nevertheless, **a recent review of the empirical evidence and theory by Lange and Topel (2006) concludes that there is little proof that the social rate of return could be lower than the private rate of return on schooling.** The evidence indicates that education raises human capital, which raises productivity, confirming the efficiency rationale for education.

The review of existing literature on economic returns to education conducted for this study, as well as previous reviews (see Psacharopoulos and Patrinos 2004), revealed a wide range of estimates and empirical approaches for estimating the actual causal effect of education on earnings. **The more significant patterns observed in the literature include the following:**

- The highest returns on education are observed in low- and middle-income countries where the educational attainment of the population is still low (see table 3.2).
- In some low-income countries, especially in rural settings, the returns on education are very low, which suggests the existence of wage distortions in the employment that is available.
- As countries reach a higher level of economic development and their inhabitants attain a higher level of education, the returns to education begin to fall.
- The private returns to higher education, especially for men, are increasing at a higher rate than those to other educational levels. Because limited access to higher education is still a reality in many countries, higher education could actually work to worsen the distribution of income in these countries.
- Women still garner higher returns to their schooling investments, especially at low educational levels.

With rapidly expanding primary education, the relative returns to various levels of education may be changing. Thus, labor market returns are no longer generally characterized by the commonly assumed concave relationship with education that implied diminishing returns to additional years of schooling, for which evidence has been found in the past (Psacharopoulos 1994). In fact, a number of studies now confirm that there is a larger return to higher levels of education than to lower levels. **For instance, countries as diverse as Brazil, Chile, Côte d'Ivoire, Ghana, Indonesia, Mexico, Pakistan, the United States, and a number of others**

Table 3.2 The coefficient on years of schooling: Rate of return, regional averages
(percent)

	Mean per capita (US$)	Years of schooling	Coefficient (percent)
Asia	5,182	8.4	9.9
Europe/Middle East/North Africa	6,299	8.8	7.1
Latin America/Caribbean	3,125	8.2	12.0
OECD	24,582	9.0	7.5
Sub-Saharan Africa	974	7.3	11.7
World	9,160	8.3	9.7

Source: Psacharopoulos and Patrinos 2004.

have recently seen an increase in returns to postsecondary education compared with primary education (see Schultz 2003; de Ferranti et al. 2003; Manacorda, Sanchez-Paramo, and Schady 2005; Kingdon and Soderbom 2007a, 2007b).

The case studies on Pakistan and Ghana illustrate divergent patterns in returns to different levels of education, as shown in table 3.3 (data is conditional on respondents being in either wage, self-, or agricultural employment). In Pakistan, the marginal returns to education are generally substantially lower for men than women in both wage and self-employment, although not in agriculture. For young people in Pakistan, the returns to primary education are much lower than the returns to subsequent levels of education. For the older age group, however, the magnitude of the difference between educational levels is not that large. For Ghana, even the marginal returns to an additional year of primary education are high for men who are self-employed. For the self-employed, then, basic education appears to be an attractive investment. However, the big payoff in Ghana is for tertiary education in wage employment, although marginal returns to tertiary education are lower for men (12.8 percent) than for women (18.0 percent) (but this gender difference is not statistically significant). Overall, however, the evidence for Ghana suggests that, with the exception of self-employed men, the returns to education are substantially higher at the highest levels of education.

Figures 3.3 and 3.4 show the relationship between education and predicted earnings for Pakistan and Ghana, respectively. In Pakistan, the returns to education for men remain lower than the returns for women, with the exception of older agricultural workers. Nevertheless, women in the country actually have much lower *levels* of earnings than men. Thus, although the slope of the education-earnings relationship is steeper for women than for men in Pakistan, the intercept of the wage regression is much higher for men. This is clear from the graphs of predicted earnings in figures 3.3a through 3.3c, where the slope of the education-earnings relationship is steeper (at least on balance) for women, but the intercept is far lower.

In Ghana, there is pronounced convexity in wage returns for both men and women (that is, higher returns to higher levels of education). Women's somewhat higher returns at secondary and tertiary education levels imply that the gender gap for waged workers narrows at higher levels of education. While there is some suggestion of convexity for women in self-employment and for both genders in agriculture, neither of these

Table 3.3 Return to an additional year of schooling by level of education and type of employment, Pakistan and Ghana

Level of schooling and type of employment	Pakistan[a]				Ghana[b]	
	Age 30 and under		Over age 30			
	Men	Women	Men	Women	Men	Women
Primary						
Wage employment	**1.4**	**9.2**	**4.7**	**15.3**	0.7	2.5
Self-employed	-3.7	3.9	2.2	6.0	**12.5**	0.4
Agriculture	**10.8**	23.8	**11.4**	7.1	-2.7	2.8
Middle school						
Wage employment	1.7	15.1	4.5	15.5	8.8	0.1
Self-employed	**9.1**	12.6	3.4	**-37.3**	-13.3	5.7
Agriculture	0.9	-16.3	10.9	-47.3	-8.1	-7.7
Secondary						
Wage employment	**6.6**	12.3	7.6	27.7	0.2	7.0
Self-employed	1.7	-25.2	10.9	**43.3**	10.9	-4.4
Agriculture	15.0	76.7	12.3	-205.3	14.6	9.4
Higher secondary						
Wage employment	5.9	4.3	5.7	8.6	n.a.	n.a.
Self-employed	4.7	**69.1**	14.6	37.5	n.a.	n.a.
Agriculture	-14.0	-142.6	10.5	..	n.a.	n.a.
Tertiary						
Wage employment	**17.7**	19.9	**14.4**	-13.1	12.8	18.0
Self-employed	26.1	-9.1	6.1	101.6	-7.3	10.5
Agriculture	27.5	50.6	**57.2**	..	7.1	1.1

Source: Estimated from the Pakistan Integrated Household Survey 2001–02 and Ghana Living Standards Survey 1998 (Kingdon and Soderbom 2007a, 2007b). See appendix 2 for summary of methodology.

Note: .. = not estimated because no values in data sets; n.a. = Not applicable. Bold numbers indicate that the marginal return to education at a given level of education differs in a statistically significantly manner from the marginal return at the education level immediately below it.

a. For Pakistan, the marginal return on a year of primary schooling is calculated as the coefficient on the primary school dummy variable divided by 5, because there are 5 years in the primary school cycle. The marginal return to a year of middle-level schooling is calculated as the coefficient on the middle school dummy minus the coefficient on the primary school dummy, divided by 3, because there are 3 years in the middle school cycle (grades 6, 7, and 8); and so on for other levels of education.

b. For Ghana, the marginal return to a year of primary schooling is calculated as the coefficient on the primary school dummy variable divided by 6, because there are 6 years in the primary school cycle. The marginal return to a year of middle-level schooling is calculated as the coefficient on the middle school dummy minus the coefficient on the primary school dummy, divided by 3, because there are 3 years in the middle school cycle (grades 7, 8, and 9); and so on for other levels of education. Both secondary and tertiary levels of education are assumed to be 3-year cycles.

Figure 3.3   Predicted earnings and level of education, Pakistan

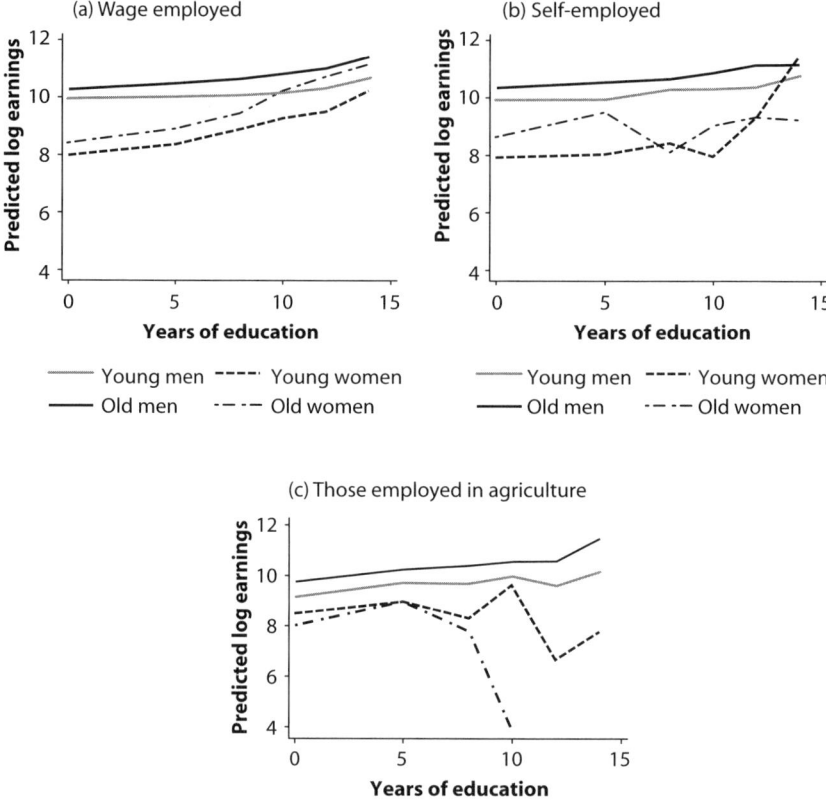

Source: Kingdon and Soderbom (2007b) using data from Pakistan Integrated Household Survey 2001–02.

indications is statistically robust. **These findings mean that in countries in which the highest returns to education accrue only to the higher levels of education, rapidly increasing education only at lower education levels will not raise earnings substantially and will not prove to be an effective means of poverty alleviation in wage employment.**

Higher returns to postbasic education in Pakistan and Ghana and a number of other countries could be explained by one of two underlying

Figure 3.4   Predicted earnings and level of education, Ghana

Source: Kingdon and Soderbom (2007a), using data from Ghana Living Standards Survey 1998.

conditions. **First, returns to higher education are likely to increase if the supply of better-educated workers grows more slowly than the derived demand for these workers** (Acemoglu 2002). This gap between demand and supply may result from a skills-biased technical change, a change in the openness of an economy that increased FDI, or specific institutional changes.[7] Because different countries are at different stages of economic development, one or more of these factors may explain the convex profile of educational returns.

Second, returns to primary education are likely to be lower if the quality of primary education is low. Despite higher basic education completion rates, fewer individuals might be acquiring the skill sets in demand by the labor market. The World Development Report 2007 (World Bank 2006), for example, suggests that although curricula and teaching methods have remained largely unchanged in developing countries over the years, employers are demanding strong thinking, communication, and entrepreneurial skills—a demand largely unmet by educational systems in the developing and transition economies.

The implications of a convex relationship between levels of education and labor market returns are considerable, and include, first, the possibility that subsidized postbasic education might contribute to, rather than alleviate, income inequality. For instance, Schultz (2003) suggests that in countries where public subsidies to postbasic education are high, as in a number of African countries, convexity suggests that the high level of public transfers made to students enrolled at this level of education benefits students whose families were relatively better educated in the past.[8] In such cases, education policies contribute to sustaining income inequality.

Second, existing education and labor market policy is predicated on the assumption that returns to education are greatest at the primary level and progressively lower at secondary and tertiary levels. The Millennium Development Goals (MDGs) also assume that the completion of basic education, along with the attainment of the other MDGs, will help realize the goal of halving the number of people living in poverty by 2015. **If, however, the relationship between education and earnings is convex (or even linear), increasing education only at low education levels will not raise earnings substantially and alone will not prove an effective means of helping people to overcome poverty.**[9]

Both of these findings indicate that a more efficient allocation of educational resources might be needed to reduce income inequality in developing countries. Most of the studies cited to this point based their analyses on estimates of the average rates of return to education, that is, on measuring returns for the mean individual with mean characteristics. However, **returns to education can be heterogeneous across people, a finding that has implications for the inequality-reducing role of education.** For instance, for varying reasons some individuals may benefit more from the same level of education. A policy maker would be interested in being able to discern such differential impacts for effective policy making.

A number of studies have investigated if and how schooling affects the conditional distribution of earnings at different points in the wage distribution. **Quantile regression (QR) analysis is a useful tool for examining the way in which the contribution of schooling varies along the earnings distribution.** Increasing returns as one goes from the lower to the higher end of the earnings distribution can be interpreted as indicating that ability and education complement each other, with more-able workers benefiting more (through higher earnings) from additional investment in education. However, a negative relationship between ability and returns to education (decreasing returns as earnings quantiles increase) suggests that education and ability are substitutes. Finally, if there is no distinct pattern, average returns (in the absence of estimation biases) capture the overall profitability of education.

The estimation of returns to education using QR is more informative than the mere statement that, on average, one more year of education results in a certain percentage increase in earnings; QR can investigate how wages vary with education at the 25th (low), 50th (median), and 75th (high) percentiles of the distribution of earnings. To the extent that observations close to the 75th percentile are accepted as indicative of higher "ability" than lower percentiles (on the grounds that such observations have atypically high wages, given their characteristics), **quantile regressions are informative of the effect of education on earnings across individuals with varying ability.**[10]

There is now a body of literature investigating the pattern of returns to an additional year of education along the earnings distribution using QR analysis. For instance, Martins and Pereira (2004) examined quantile returns for a number of European countries for a single year in the 1990s and found that the returns increased by each quantile for all countries except Greece, for which returns decreased moderately.[11] Patrinos, Ridao-Cano, and Sakellariou (2006) found that returns increased with quantiles for eight Latin American countries. However, in seven out of eight East Asian countries analyzed in the study, returns decrease by quantiles. Patrinos and colleagues suggest that **differences in the documented patterns of returns to educational levels can be linked to the different developmental stages of individual countries. Therefore, differential returns to the same levels of education might be a result of job mobility in developed countries, scarcity of skills in developing countries, differential exposure to market forces, and differential access to quality education.**[12]

Such studies have important policy implications. For instance, do poor individuals earn lower returns on the same level of education than the rich? If so, could it be because the poor have access only to poor-quality schooling? In this case, the quality of schools the poor attend needs to be improved. Successful policies that have improved access to better quality schools for the poor include vouchers[13] and public-private partnerships to provide quality education to underserved areas,[14] among others. Yet, **poor individuals might earn lower returns on the same level of education because individuals with characteristics other than schooling, such as ability and motivation, tend to benefit more from education**—skills tend to beget skills (di Gropello 2006). This result generally occurs when labor markets are sufficiently competitive. For instance, Patrinos and Ridao-Cano (2006) suggest that the more competitive a job market, the more likely it is that increasing returns to education by quantiles will be observed. **In such cases, governments may choose to emphasize the development of skills other than basic cognitive skills, either in schools or through external mentoring programs for young individuals.** The need to acquire behavioral or communication skills might, moreover, be particularly high among children from low socioeconomic backgrounds.

Turning to the case studies of Ghana and Pakistan, QR analysis uncovers differing patterns of returns to schooling by earnings quantile, both between the two countries and between genders in each country (see tables 3.4a and 3.4b).

The results for Ghana show that for both men and women, there is a consistent pattern of different returns to education in wage employment at different points of the conditional earnings distribution. Returns to education are highest in the lowest earnings group (bottom quantile) and lowest in the highest earnings group (top quantile). For both men and women, the difference between the top and bottom quantiles is statistically significant, although the size of the difference is nearly twice as big for women as for men. Similar results are obtained for self-employed women, for whom returns to education in the top earnings quantile are significantly lower than those in the bottom earnings quantile—a difference of 8 percentage points. Thus, in these occupation groups, people with lower ability appear to have higher rates of return to education, lending support to the notion that education can be substituted for low ability. **The analysis suggests that among men and women who are wage earners and among self-employed women, education in Ghana is**

Table 3.4a Earnings and years of schooling, quantile regressions, Ghana

	Wage employed	Self-employed	Agriculture
Men			
Education	**0.058**	0.033	0.014
(25th percentile of earnings)			
Education	**0.049**	**0.042**	0.013
(50th percentile of earnings)			
Education	**0.042**	**0.079**	-0.006
(75th percentile of earnings)			
Women			
Education	**0.081**	**0.034**	0.013
(25th percentile of earnings)			
Education	**0.066**	-0.002	**0.026**
(50th percentile of earnings)			
Education	**0.053**	-0.046	**0.032**
(75th percentile of earnings)			

Source: Kingdon and Soderbom 2007a.

Note: Age, age squared, and province dummy variables are included in all regressions. Values in bold are statistically significant.

Table 3.4b Earnings and years of schooling, quantile regressions, Pakistan

	Wage employed		Self-employed		Agriculture	
	Men	Women	Men	Women	Men	Women
Young (30 and under)						
Education	**0.036**	**0.164**	**0.043**	**0.061**	**0.067**	0.102
(25th percentile of earnings)						
Education	**0.036**	**0.153**	**0.048**	**0.090**	**0.077**	**0.083**
(50th percentile of earnings)						
Education	**0.034**	**0.138**	**0.049**	**0.064**	**0.055**	0.013
(75th percentile of earnings)						
Old (over 30)						
Education	**0.068**	**0.226**	**0.051**	**0.059**	**0.094**	-0.037
(25th percentile of earnings)						
Education	**0.061**	**0.190**	**0.055**	**0.042**	**0.082**	0.023
(50th percentile of earnings)						
Education	**0.063**	**0.149**	**0.065**	-0.166	**0.077**	0.001
(75th percentile of earnings)						

Source: Kingdon and Soderbom 2007b.

Note: Age, age squared, and province dummy variables are included in all regressions. Values in bold are statistically significant.

inequality reducing, because education lowers the wage differences between low- and high-ability individuals. Among self-employed men, however, education appears to be inequality increasing: the return to education in the top earnings quantile is nearly double the return in the median quantile, which is weakly higher than the return to education in the bottom quantile. No such patterns are discernible in agriculture.

The results for Pakistan (table 3.4b) indicate that for women in wage employment, returns to education are highest in the lowest earnings group (bottom quantile) and lowest in the highest group (the top quantile). Those with lower ability appear to have higher rates of return to education. This finding is true for both younger and older age groups among women, suggesting that for women wage earners education is inequality reducing because it reduces the wage differences between low- and high-ability individuals.

Conclusions

Education continues to yield high returns to individuals in the labor market. Even basic literacy and numeracy provide very high returns. However, **there is an urgent need to improve the quality of education in developing countries, particularly at lower levels.** If the attainment of basic skills requires 8 to 12 years of education, as is the case in Pakistan and Ghana, the education system is extremely inefficient. Moreover, if a 15-year-old student enrolled in school is unable to use the literacy skills he or she has acquired at lower levels of schooling to attain further knowledge (as indicated by a low proficiency score on the PISA reading assessment), the education system has failed the student.

Improving the quality of education requires improving the efficiency of educational spending, which means focusing on institutions (see Hanushek and Woessmann 2007). Although evidence of a convex education-earnings profile indicates that investments in lower levels of education do not help the poor climb out of poverty, this finding seems more likely to reflect the fact that **primary education alone is not equipping individuals with skills that are highly rewarded in the labor market (critical thinking, problem solving, and behavioral skills, as well as skills in information technology).**

The heterogeneity of labor market outcomes for individuals with the same level of education emphasizes the fact that not all individuals benefit equally from education. In some instances, education appears to substitute for lack of ability, thus benefiting low-ability individuals. However, depending on the country context, this pattern could be caused by wage distortions created by government labor policies. These findings lead to a number of policy implications for educational specialists that are discussed in chapter 5.

With respect to Ghana and Pakistan, it is revealing that these developing countries show different patterns in returns to education. **In Pakistan, high returns are seen at all levels of education, particularly among women in wage employment (the better-remunerated occupation group), and these increase at higher levels of education, whereas higher returns are apparent only at the highest level of education in Ghana.** These findings indicate that education is inequality reducing in Pakistan, but risks becoming inequality producing in Ghana at higher levels if these levels are accessible only to the elite of the country. The policy implications of these findings strengthen the case for public investment in the education of women at all levels in Pakistan, and for targeting public investment at the higher levels of education in Ghana to the poor and the talented.

Notes

1. These articles are summarized in appendix 3. The advantages of using test scores over self-reported measures to determine cognitive achievement include better individual assessment and standardization, which controls for varying quality across schools (Jolliffe 1998). However, such tests and data are not readily available in most low-income countries, particularly for a large nationally representative group. Self-reported literacy and numeracy thus serve as a (possibly noisy) proxy.

2. Glewwe (2002) suggests that most of these studies have some data or estimation problems; therefore, their conventional estimated results must be treated with caution.

3. It appears from table 3.1 that individuals in Pakistan who can read and write are more likely to be unemployed than in wage employment. This finding could be the result of people with education having to queue for appropriate jobs, therefore making them more likely to be in the unemployed pool of the labor force.

4. While in common literature the term "returns" is used, strictly speaking, the coefficients estimated using Mincerian-type earnings functions simply represent the gross earnings premium of being literate or numerate compared with

not possessing these skills; it is thus not the return itself because it does not take into account the cost of attaining these skills.

5. See Kingdon and Soderbom (2007a, 2007b) for details on estimation.

6. These countries include Argentina, Azerbaijan, Brazil, Bulgaria, Colombia, Indonesia, the Kyrgyz Republic, Montenegro, Qatar, Romania, Serbia, and Tunisia (OECD 2007).

7. These issues remain underresearched, particularly with respect to the education and skills development of the supply of labor (see Schultz 2003; Manacorda, Sanchez-Paramo, and Schady 2005).

8. Mainly because of low intergenerational educational mobility, people who are less educated are less likely to have children who are highly educated (King 1997; Schultz 2003).

9. This does not mean that basic education should not be subsidized—it should be highly subsidized everywhere because countries with low levels of education will otherwise remain trapped in technological stagnation and low growth (de Ferranti et al. 2003).

10. One caveat is that the QR approach is useful for determining the returns to education for people at different levels of ability only if it is assumed that education is exogenous. However, one cannot assume a priori that education is exogenous. Thus, it cannot be said that the return to education for, say, the 90th percentile, gives the true return to education for high-ability people, purged of ability bias. The same caution is given in Arias, Hallock, and Sosa-Escudero (2001), who cite QR studies of returns to education (Buchinsky 1994; Machado and Mata 2000; Mwabu and Schultz 1996), noting that the results of these studies should be interpreted with caution because they do not handle the problems of endogeneity bias.

11. The countries examined in the study included Austria, Denmark, Finland, France, Ireland, Italy, Netherlands, Norway, Portugal, Spain, Sweden, Switzerland, and the United Kingdom. The authors explain the result for Greece as an outcome of progressive taxation, which has a stronger impact on eroding returns to education at the top of the earnings distribution than at the bottom.

12. Ethiopia is one of the few low-income countries for which evidence exists on the heterogeneity of ability, with one study finding that education is more beneficial to the less able (Girma and Kedir 2005).

13. Angrist, Bettinger, and Kremer (2006) provide interesting evidence on the impact of vouchers in Colombia.

14. See Barrera-Osorio (2007) on public-private partnerships in the Bogotá schools program.

CHAPTER 4

Employment Outcomes and Links to the Broader Economic Context

A holistic picture of education–labor market linkages requires that the demand for labor be analyzed. Chapter 3 focused on education outcomes mainly from the supply side of the equation. However, a substantial part of the framework developed in chapter 2 cannot be explained simply by education outcomes because wage dispersion is not the result of human capital alone. **It is important to discern what proportions of observed wage dispersion are due to unobservable worker skills (efficiency wages), job-matching frictions, or other labor market inefficiencies, because these factors have important policy implications.** For instance, if unobservable skills of the worker are the key to wage differentials, then education and training would be the principal policy avenues to improve incomes. However, if wage differentials are the result of a sorting process among firms, the key policy issues would involve changes in the industrial structure of an economy (Sandefur, Teal, and Serneels 2006).

Demand-Side Analysis

The demand for labor is a derived demand. This demand has two dimensions important for policy. **The first dimension deals with the types of jobs that are created as demand expands.** This dimension identifies relevant policy issues as arising in markets other than the labor market. **The second dimension focuses on whether there is a policy problem in how the labor market is operating.** This dimension requires the analyst to focus on supply-side issues, including the match between the supply of and demand for skills, the link between the wages paid by a firm or employer and its productivity, and the role of labor market regulation in limiting the willingness of firms to hire. The two approaches are complementary and very directly linked.

One common approach to analyzing the first dimension of labor demand is to estimate the types of jobs created in an economy, together with how these jobs are linked to the expansion (or contraction) of the economy. The sectoral breakdown of a multitopic household survey, such as the Living Standards Measurement Survey, or a labor force survey can provide the necessary data. Repeated cross-sections can be used to shed light on the shift in relative demand for education over time by analyzing changes in the relative supply of workers with different education levels and the relative returns to these levels.[1]

To analyze the second dimension of labor demand, the factors that affect labor demand in individual sectors must be determined. To understand the number and type of jobs in demand—the critical issue for policy makers—a different kind of information base is needed, ideally, firm-level surveys.[2]

Thus, to gain a comprehensive picture of the demand side for skills and education in labor markets, the following issues need to be researched, based on a combination of data sources such as multitopic household surveys, labor force surveys, firm-level surveys, information from relevant national ministries, and tracer studies that follow cohorts of education graduates in labor markets over time.

- **Formal and informal job creation.** Depending on the country context, it is crucial to identify where job creation has taken place, that is, informal versus formal sector, public versus private sector, and so forth. The Ghana country study, for example, shows that over the last two decades, nonfarm self-employment and jobs in small firms exploded relative to jobs in the formal sector.[3] While the number of firms with more than 100 employees scarcely changed over the period from 1987 to 2003, the number of firms with fewer than five employees increased from 2,884 to 14,353.

- **Education and earnings in formal and informal jobs.** The creation and destruction of jobs in various sectors has important repercussions on the types of education and skill sets demanded in labor markets. In Ghana, for instance, the public sector and large firms show the greatest demand for skills gained through formal education and experience acquired on the job. The changing pattern of labor demand toward small firms and self-employment, however, implies a reduction in the demand for such skilled employees. And, although the earnings in self-employment are comparable to wage earnings in small firms, they are substantially less than those in the formal sector. The returns to both education and training, where training is measured by general work experience and tenure in the job, are thus lower in the self-employed urban sector than in wage employment in Ghana.
- **Labor regulations and unionization in dominant sectors of employment.** To understand the demand for labor in an economy, the hiring and firing rules in the dominant employment sectors must be understood (for example, whether an employment guarantee exists for certain occupations), as must be minimum wage laws, employee protection regulations, and taxation. Unionization of the labor force and the way in which negotiations take place between employers and unions can be critical for determining labor market outcomes, even including the value of particular skills and education.
- **The macroeconomic context.** Last, it is extremely important to take into account the overall macroeconomic context of an economy to understand the demand for labor. Jobs, particularly good jobs, are dependent on a number of enabling factors, including the investment climate, capital flows, and financial markets, among others. The prices of raw materials for the manufacturing sector, the exchange rate for the trading industry, the policies on foreign direct investment, and the level of technological advancement will all determine which skill sets, and how much of each, are demanded in the labor markets.

Skills Mismatch

Information asymmetries in labor markets can send the wrong signals to firms and individuals seeking employment. Under such conditions, differences between the demand for education by households and by firms create a skills mismatch.[4] The skills mismatch in labor markets can manifest as (i) unemployment or underemployment of an educated labor force (Monk, Sandefur, and Teal 2007; Nielsen 2007); (ii) a shortage of skilled labor resulting from inadequate education (Cruz-Castro and Conlon 2001; Diaz, Saavedra, and Torero 2004; AFESD 2003); or (iii) migration (Nielsen 2007; Alofs 2002).[5]

Different macroeconomic and country contexts create very different labor market demands and associated rewards. In Ghana, for instance, apprenticeship appears to be the most important form of skills development and the people who benefit most from it possess a lower secondary education (Monk, Sandefur, and Teal 2007). Evidence suggests that there is a 41 percent increase in the wages of people who enter the labor market as apprentices with the lowest levels of education. However, no such increase is observed for individuals entering the apprenticeship labor market with postsecondary education. In Mongolia, a very different set of skills needs to be developed in students, but starting from a low base because the transitioning nature of the economy requires thinking and behavioral skills as well as practical English, information technology skills, and technical skills. In Mongolia, 30 percent of firms list lack of appropriate skills and education as a severe constraint. Furthermore, 93 percent of workers from these same firms state that they lack creative thinking and behavioral skills (World Bank 2007). Such information highlights the lag in changes in education policy and demand for education, both by individuals and firms.

The current global economy values individuals who, in addition to basic cognitive skills, have core competencies in critical thinking, problem solving, and entrepreneurship. These skills give students the foundation for operating successfully in any sector of the economy. Unfortunately, the primary education systems of most developing countries do not develop these skills in students, creating a very real skills mismatch. In fact, a tracer study following postsecondary education school leavers in certain Sub-Saharan African countries identified critical thinking and problem-solving skills as the critical factors missing in their education (Al-Samarrai and Bennell 2007). Informal markets, including self-employment, are usually the employer of last resort for individuals not finding employment in the formal sector. Yet, as research in Africa has shown, the informal market is not necessarily limited to low skills and traditional mechanisms. It is, in fact, a dynamic market in many countries, responding to the needs of changing economies by, for example, creating a new breed of young entrepreneurs who operate Internet cafes in many African countries (Johanson and Adams 2004).

Transition and developed economies in particular demonstrate greater demand for more general skills that can easily be adapted to the changing needs of industry, given that specific technical skills may become obsolete very rapidly. According to a study on Britain and Spain, general skills have become increasingly valuable in labor markets characterized by change, in which there is a constant need to adapt to new developments in technology and working methods. In light of the pace of technological innovation, the value of overly narrow vocational qualifications is accordingly diminishing (Cruz-Castro and Conlon 2001). See box 4.1 on attempts to remedy skill mismatches.

A shift from manufacturing to services and research-oriented firms in the transition economies of Bulgaria, Poland, and the Russian Federation created a skills mismatch that led to high unemployment during the 1990s. A study on Russia, for example, found high and rising demand for educated and highly skilled labor in the services and research industries (Lukyanova et al. 2007). Similarly, in Bulgaria, the risk of losing a job or being unemployed was highest and longest among workers with lower education or vocational or technical education, while those with easily adaptable skills were most likely to be employed or to find new employment within a year (Rutkowski 2003). An examination of labor market conditions in the Slovak Republic reveals a similar scenario: while unemployment increased for all levels of education, those with secondary or lower education fared the worst (Revenga et al. 2002).

Interlinkages with Other Markets

As mentioned, the demand for labor is a derived demand affected by at least two factors: policies that affect how the labor market operates and policies that affect how markets other than the labor market operate, including those that address macroeconomic stability, trade, FDI, and the like. **If the major issues that affect education–labor market linkages originate in the demand side of the labor market, further expansion of education is unwarranted without attempting to address these issues.** For example, subsidies in tertiary education need to be accompanied by the creation of an environment conducive to investment and technological progress. In the absence of such an environment, countries will find their

Box 4.1

Correcting the skills mismatch: Mixed outcomes of youth labor market interventions

Any policy that aims to support individuals as they enter the labor market by providing them the right skills mix needs to be aligned with the socioeconomic conditions of that particular market. A global inventory of active labor market interventions around the world that support young workers shows that the highest numbers of interventions are related to skills training (Betcherman et al. 2007). Of the 289 programs reviewed, 98 provided vocational training, including through apprenticeship. The inventory suggests that evaluation of such programs is weak and that the absence of rigorous impact studies causes policy makers to overestimate their effects. In addition, most programs do not appear to be cost effective. Overall, the study emphasizes the importance of flexible labor markets for achieving better impact for youth-focused interventions.[a]

Betcherman, Olivas, and Dar (2004) found that labor market information services in general have a positive impact on labor market outcomes, given favorable economic conditions in a country. Labor market training for the unemployed also appears effective if it is job-specific practical training. In contrast, class-based training schemes for the long-term unemployed do not have a positive impact on labor market outcomes, a finding that highlights the importance of appropriate program design.

(continued)

populations emigrating for better opportunities and governments will need to continue subsidizing education to compensate for weak effective demand (de Ferranti et al. 2003).

Using the country study on Ghana,[6] the discussion in chapter 3 indicates that tertiary education raises earnings mainly in wage employment. It does not *directly* raise earnings for the large majority of workers in Ghana, however, because self-employment and agriculture together constitute 82.5 percent of the employed workforce and the returns to education in both occupations are very low. Thus, **while it might seem that the economic incentives for acquiring schooling are weak in Ghana, it is clear that education helps individuals enter the more lucrative part of the labor market.** To obtain a more comprehensive picture of education–

Box 4.1

Continued

The picture of labor market interventions in general is mixed. An early randomized study of a U.S. program designed to help disadvantaged workers (LaLonde 1986), for example, showed a positive impact on participants' earnings. The study also emphasized the need for randomized evaluation of such programs because econometric analysis and comparison groups do not yield precise estimates. One of the latest randomized studies, conducted in Colombia, found that a program for the two lowest socioeconomic strata of the population raised earnings and employment for both men and women, with larger effects on women (Attanasio, Kugler, and Meghir 2007). A cost-benefit analysis of the results suggested that the program generates large net gains, with internal rates of return of about 13.5 percent for women and 4.5 percent for men. "Jovenes" (youth) programs—which target disadvantaged youth with a combination of training and work experience, plus other services, such as psychological development—also showed positive outcomes in the short term in certain Latin American countries, including Argentina, Chile, Peru, and Uruguay (Betcherman, Olivas, and Dar 2004).

Source: Attanasio, Kugler, and Meghir 2007; Betcherman et al. 2007; Betcherman, Olivas, and Dar 2004; Dar and Tzannatos 1999; LaLonde 1986.

a. Another, earlier study (Dar and Tzannatos 1999) suggested that training programs for youth might not be very effective, given their poor track record.

labor market linkages, however, job creation and destruction, and how they are related to the macroeconomic context, must be considered.

As noted earlier in this chapter, the pattern of job creation in Ghana has overwhelmingly favored nonfarm self-employment and jobs in small firms rather than jobs in the formal sector (defined here as the public sector and firms with more than 100 employees) over the last two decades. **While the number of firms in Ghana with more than 100 employees scarcely changed over the period from 1987 to 2003, the number of firms with fewer than 5 employees increased almost 500 percent** (from 2,884 to 14,353). At the same time, Teal (2007) reports that 1987–88 to 1998–99, the labor force in Ghana increased from 6.5 to 8.8 million, while the number of wage employees scarcely changed (growing from 1.12 million to 1.17 million). The number classified as unemployed in household surveys meanwhile increased only by 200,000. Among the remainder of jobs created during the period, half were in the rural sector and half were in nonfarm self-employment.

Because the Ghana country study shows very low returns to education in agriculture,[7] the discussion here focuses on the manufacturing sector in Ghana, both for the self-employed and wage employees, to determine the extent to which education might be the binding constraint on low incomes.[8] Two important issues become apparent. First, as seen in figure 4.1, a very large wage difference exists between types of labor. Second, wages are higher in larger firms (see figure 4.2), a finding that remains true even when the results are controlled for the observed skills of workers in firms.[9] **That is, the rise in wages in larger firms does not reflect the fact that larger firms tend to employ more workers with more education.**

If educated people are getting good returns in the manufacturing sector and returns are higher in larger firms, why has the larger manufacturing sector not expanded to absorb the labor supply? The Ghana Manufacturing and Enterprise Survey, which asks firms about the constraints they face, sheds light on the answer. **Ghanaian firms mentioned the following constraints as their three most important problems: access to credit, lack of demand for their goods, and access to and the cost of raw materials.** All three issues were reported more frequently by smaller than by larger firms (see table 4.1).

Lack of appropriate skills appears to be the least important reported constraint for Ghanaian firms. This finding is in sharp contrast to findings

Figure 4.1   Wages per month by skill level, Ghana manufacturing sector

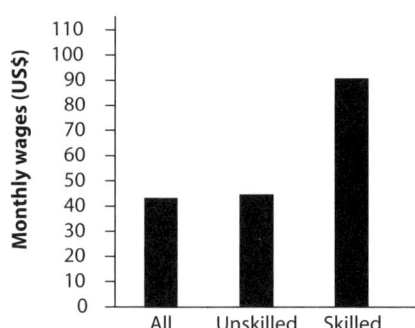

Source: Teal 2007.

Figure 4.2   Wages per month by firm size, Ghana manufacturing sector

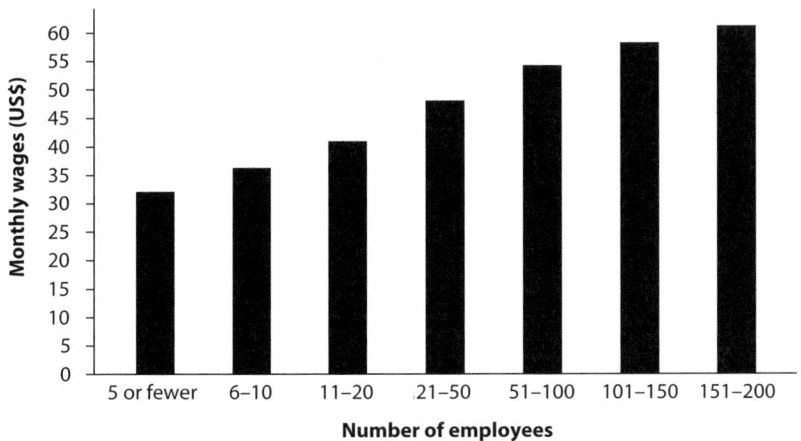

Source: Teal 2007.

Note: The wages are calculated for an average worker over the period 1992 to 2003 with the average amount of human capital measured by gender, age, education, and tenure.

from enterprise surveys in most countries. As seen in table 4.2, a substantial number of firms in countries worldwide report that lack of appropriate skills and education are a severe constraint. A tracer study that followed secondary school and university leavers in four Sub-Saharan African countries reported, moreover, that lack of entrepreneurial skills was an important constraint in the creation of a viable private sector (Al-Samarrai and Bennell 2007). The study also reported that the individuals in the tracer analysis had demanded revisions to the curricula in their respective countries to focus them more on practical and vocational aspects.

The analysis of Ghana thus suggests that there is an adequate or excess supply of the skills required in the labor market for the types of firms and jobs that are emerging in its economy, that is, nonfarm self-employment and small-scale firms. To complete the picture, however, the macroeconomic context of the country must be considered (see figure 2.1).

One major constraint noted repeatedly by firms in Ghana is access to and cost of raw materials. This constraint was not identified in many other African firm-level surveys. Some of the most striking changes in Ghana between the late 1990s and early 2000s are seen in figure 4.3, which

Table 4.1 Selected firm problems by firm size, Ghana, 2002
(percentage of firms reporting each problem)

Firm size	Access to credit	Demand	Cost of domestic raw materials	Access to domestic raw materials	Taxes	Inflation	High interest rates	Lack of skilled labor
Large	6	6	19	19	25	13	6	6
Medium	26	19	26	23	14	2	21	0
Small	64	16	32	11	5	9	2	2
Micro	47	53	33	7	13	0	7	0
Total	40	20	28	16	12	6	10	2

Source: Teal 2007.

Note: Micro has fewer than five employees; small has between 5 and 20; medium has 21 to 100; large has more than 100.

Table 4.2 When skills are scarce: Sample responses from select economies, various years
(percentage of firms reporting each problem as a major constraint)

Country	Firm size	Tax rates	Access to and cost of finance	Labor skill level
Egypt, Arab Rep. of (2004)	Small (1–19 employees)	86	38	24
	Medium (20–99 employees)	74	41	21
	Large (100+ employees)	73	31	19
Ghana (2007)	Small (1–19 employees)	27	69	6
	Medium (20–99 employees)	32	68	3
	Large (100+ employees)	53	42	1
India (2002)	Small (1–19 employees)	26	18	12
	Medium (20–99 employees)	29	22	13
	Large (100+ employees)	28	15	14
Indonesia (2003)	Small (1–19 employees)	0	25	12
	Medium (20–99 employees)	19	16	13
	Large (100+ employees)	40	19	24
Mongolia (2004)	Small (1–19 employees)	63	40	25
	Medium (20-99 employees)	72	38	32
	Large (100+ employees)	60	33	37
Pakistan (2002)	Small (1–19 employees)	36	34	9
	Medium (20–99 employees)	50	41	16
	Large (100+ employees)	57	32	13
Russian Fed. (2005)	Small (1–19 employees)	25	15	10
	Medium (20–99 employees)	20	13	17
	Large (100+ employees)	18	6	14

Source: Enterprise Survey Database, World Bank.

shows the macroeconomic background against which firms were operating. The nominal exchange rate, for example, fell from about 2,000 Ghanaian cedis per U.S. dollar in the late 1990s to 8,000 cedis by the time data was collected in 2003.[10] The domestic price level change over this period, however, was relatively modest. As a result, there was a massive fall in the real exchange rate (RER), shown in figure 4.3b.[11] The massive nominal devaluation effected a real devaluation of 60 percent. In 2000, this measure of the RER registered its lowest point of the period 1990 to 2003.

Figure 4.3   The macroeconomic background in Ghana, 1990–2003

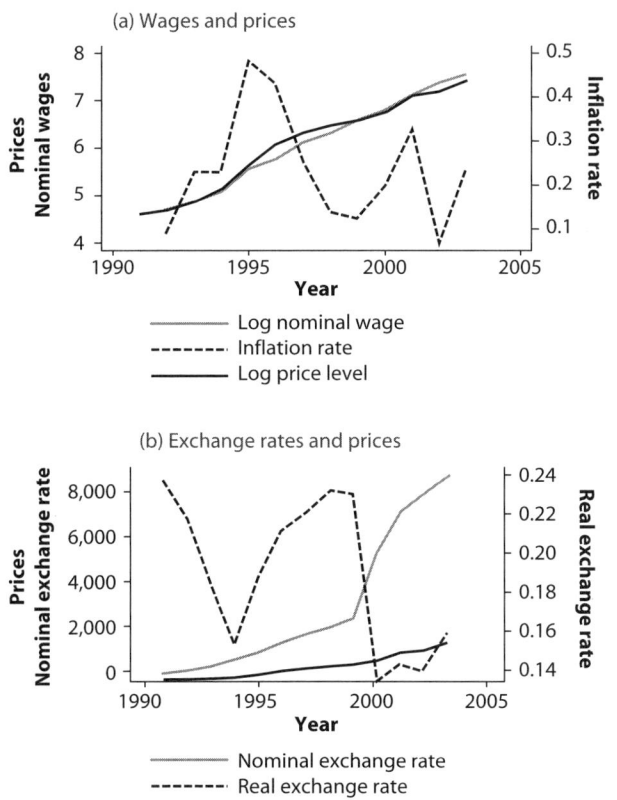

Source: Teal (2007) using data from the Ghana Institute of Statistical, Social and Economic Research (2000) and earlier publications.

The large rise in the price of imports relative to domestic prices makes the increasing concern about the cost of raw materials readily understandable (the price of raw materials is closely related to the price of imports). **Firms see themselves squeezed between rising costs and limited demand. Barring access to credit, they cannot expand the scale of their operations.**

Thus, keeping figure 4.3 in mind aids the understanding of table 4.1, that is, demand is only a major issue if the firm is dependent on the domestic market for its sales and is of lesser concern to exporting firms that use domestic inputs. However, the situation is quite different with respect to the cost of and access to domestic raw materials. Access to domestic raw materials is more important for medium and large firms than it is for small and micro ones. While cost is less of a concern for large firms it is a much bigger concern for them than is access to credit.

Policies aimed at improving the skills of the workforce will have very limited impact on the incomes of those who acquire the skills, or on the performance of the economy, unless policies are also in place that increase the demand for these skills. In Ghana at present, increases in the demand for labor come overwhelmingly from the domestic market, where there has been a far more rapid expansion of self-employment than wage employment. As seen in earlier sections of this report, the return to skills at low levels of education is very low in Ghana. These two facts are linked. While demand for low-educated labor fails to rise as fast as the supply, the price of skilled workers will inevitably be high. While improving the quality and amount of educational skills is part of the policy package required from government, it is only part—the package will fail unless the issue of job creation is addressed within the broader macroeconomic context.

Conclusions

Education is an important catalyst for improving the livelihood of individuals, with evidence showing positive returns to education in various sectors of the economy, including agriculture and nonwage sectors. However, **the right labor market policies, as well as trade and industrial policies, need to be in place to create effective demand for educated workers.** If, for instance, the education system provides good incentives and subsidies for individuals to achieve good-quality higher education, it is important that the economy is positioned to benefit from FDI and trade openness, which can stimulate competitiveness and lead to technological advancement in firms.

The analysis in this chapter has highlighted the importance of a comprehensive, multisectoral approach to analyzing the demand for education in the labor market. It has also emphasized the need to streamline education policies so that the supply of skills and education matches demand in the labor market. A number of studies at the World Bank are moving toward such a comprehensive approach to skill gaps and market needs. One effort is "MILES:" Macroeconomic framework, Investment climate and institutions, Labor market regulations, Education and skills, and Social protection. Currently being implemented in a few countries, MILES uses comprehensive analysis of education–labor market linkages to develop policies that foster job creation and poverty reduction.

The framework within which educational supply and demand are analyzed thus needs to be broadened to include a country's macroeconomic situation, investment climate, and labor market policies. A more comprehensive framework will not only strengthen the diagnostic capacity of education supply and demand analysis, it will make the policy approach to education issues more efficient.

Notes

1. For a detailed methodology, see Katz and Murphy (1992).
2. See appendix 1 for a more extended discussion of this topic.
3. Defined as the public sector and firms with more than 100 employees.
4. For further discussion, see Adams, Greig, and McQuaid (2000); Alofs (2002); Halaby (1994); Katz and Stark (1987).
5. In addition, both developed and developing economies can experience the phenomenon of over-education. Scandinavian countries, for instance, have an oversupply of highly educated labor, especially among immigrant labor. **A recent study of the Danish labor market found that at least 25 percent of the male immigrant population is overeducated, compared with 15 percent of native Danes.** There is, moreover, a relative penalty for this overqualification: while years of overeducation do increase wages, this increase is much less than the wage increase for those with adequate years of education. The penalty is thus even larger for overeducated immigrants than overeducated Danes (Nielsen 2007).
6. This section draws only on the Ghana case study and not on Pakistan because

of the existence of data from the Ghana Manufacturing and Enterprise Survey for multiple years from the 1990s to 2005.

7. Most likely because of the technologically traditional nature of agriculture.

8. The results reported here come from the background paper conducted for the study by Teal (2007), using the Ghana Household Worker Survey (GHWS) and the Ghana Manufacturing Enterprise Surveys. These surveys were conducted jointly by the Ghana Statistical Office and the Center for the Study of African Economies.

9. One potential reason is that larger firms tend to be unionized. Teal (2007) suggests that even after controlling for human capital, a large wage premium appears to be attached to union membership, though the size of the premium has decreased over the last decade.

10. The survey was conducted in 2003, thus the rate for 2002 would have been the rate that respondents had in mind during the survey.

11. The real exchange rate (RER) in figure 4.3 is defined as

$$RER = \frac{Urban\ CPI}{Xrate \times USPrices}$$

where *Xrate* is the nominal exchange rate and *USPrices* are the unit value of U.S. exports. The index is defined so that a fall in the RER is a real devaluation.

CHAPTER 5

Conclusion: How Education Can Improve Labor Market Outcomes

Education is a necessary but not sufficient condition for an individual to enjoy good labor market outcomes, whether in the formal or informal economic sectors. **In addition to education, good labor market opportunities for the skilled require an economy as a whole to be operating well, with macroeconomic stability, an attractive investment climate, and efficient labor markets, among other factors.** This report emphasizes the importance of a holistic approach to analyzing education–labor market issues, with particular stress on education market diagnosis.

Different countries at different levels of economic development have diverse requirements for education. A study by de Ferranti et al. (2003) suggested, for example, that whereas East Asian countries might benefit from more secondary school graduates to fill their skill needs gap, Latin American countries, because of their wealth of natural resources, would benefit from more experts in manufacturing processes and more tertiary education graduates.

The analysis and review in this report points to a number of strong messages for education and its role in determining labor market outcomes. First, literacy, numeracy, and basic cognitive skills improve individuals' economic outcomes, whether through the indirect effect of sorting in more lucrative occupations or the direct effect of these skills on earnings. However, **evidence suggests that it takes 8 to 12 years of schooling in developing countries, such as Ghana and Pakistan, to become functionally literate and numerate. This finding is indicative of the poor quality of learning in education systems at the primary level.** Policies that attempt to improve the quality of education, such as providing adequate pedagogical resources, textbooks, and well-trained and motivated teachers to primary schools, as well as providing school communities with accountability mechanisms to monitor the learning of their children, would go a long way toward improving learning outcomes.

Recent evidence also suggests that the earlier in childhood that investments are made in developing the cognitive skills of children, the better the long-term impacts are for learning, skills development, and labor market outcomes. It is, therefore, essential to invest in quality early childhood education. Randomized trials of early childhood development programs that support disadvantaged children have shown long-terms benefits to individuals. **Such investments, when made at an earlier age, lower the cost of later investments by making learning more efficient.** Examples of such investments include the Abecedarian program and the Perry preschool programs in the United States. **Evidence also suggests that the efficiency of education at early levels is enhanced by parallel investments in children's health.** In the developing world, for example, a large number of countries have introduced conditional cash transfers for families, provided that their young children are vaccinated, given regular health visits, and provided proper nutrition. Such programs not only help reduce the vulnerability of disadvantaged children, they tend to enhance the efficiency of early learning.

Another major finding of this report is that the shape of the education-earnings profile appears to be changing from concave, in which primary education earns the highest returns, to convex, in which secondary and tertiary educations earn the highest returns in the labor market. This changing profile has profound implications for the poverty-reducing effects of education. For instance, the Millennium Development Goals assume that the completion of basic education, along with the attainment of other MDGs, will help realize the goal of halving world poverty by 2015. **If, however, the relationship of education and earnings is convex (or even linear), then expanding enrollment only at lower levels of education will not raise earnings substantially, and consequently not prove to be an effective means of helping people out of poverty.**

Given increasing global demand for skills and the development of skills-biased technology, the returns to primary education may indeed be low. Alternatively, **the returns to primary education, especially in developing nations, could be low because the education systems are failing to produce minimum functional literacy and numeracy skills at the primary level.** In either case, the provision of high-quality subsidized primary education is warranted, not only because it empowers people and helps reduce inequality, but because countries with low levels of education are at risk of remaining trapped in technological stagnation and low growth (de Ferranti et al. 2003).

Research also suggests that not all individuals benefit from education equally, meaning that there are heterogeneous labor market outcomes. Looking at the returns to education across a conditional earnings distribution, analysis shows increasing, decreasing, or constant returns by quantiles, depending on the country. **For the limited number of countries for which evidence exists, it appears that returns to education increase by quantile in more-developed countries, and decrease in developing countries.** In an earnings equation, the unexplained variation is assumed to be explained by innate unobservable ability. Increasing returns to education as one goes from the lower to the higher end of the earnings distribution is therefore interpreted as indicating that ability and education complement each other. Whether this condition holds depends on the country context; the policy implications for heterogeneity must be interpreted in light of the broader context of a given labor market.

In a perfectly competitive labor market, skills such as motivation and ability may have higher value, thus people with higher ability may reap higher returns. From an education policy maker's point of view, **this finding supports the importance of noncognitive skill development in schools and the education system as a whole.** Certain types of mentoring programs, such as the Big Brother/Big Sister programs in the United States, may also help develop such noncognitive skills.

In countries where there are large disparities in the quality of education between the rich and the poor, and where individuals are systematically sorted into high-quality schools by wealth, the poor will attain fewer skills for the same "quantity" of education. The policy option in such a case would be to counter the sorting process through the provision of choice of better schooling through, for example, school vouchers or better-quality publicly funded private schools for the poor (Angrist, Bettinger, and Kremer 2006; Barrera-Osorio 2007). Evidence of decreasing returns from the lower to the upper end of labor market earnings can be interpreted as a positive indication that schooling can substitute for ability, that is, that education plays an inequality-reducing role. Once again, however, the country context needs to be considered before recommending policy changes because decreasing returns could also be the result of wage distortions caused by labor market rigidities.

As seen in chapter 4, **policies aimed at improving the skills of the workforce will have very limited impact on the incomes of the people who acquire them, or on the performance of the economy, unless other policies are in place that increase the demand for these skills.** In many countries, skills mismatch and overeducation cause both high unemployment and underemployment. A holistic analysis of education and labor demand, one that analyzes education in a broader macroeconomic context, helps ensure a correct diagnostic response. To ensure that education contributes to the growth of an economy, the role of FDI flows, trade penetration, and industrial policies in inducing skills-biased technological change and creating associated demand for education in the labor market needs to be better understood. **Only a multisectoral approach to education–labor market linkages will enable policy makers to focus on how demand for education increases with broader policy changes in the global economy** and how a country can ensure that it maintains a competitive workforce capable of responding to the changing needs of the economy.

Analyzing Education, Skills, and Labor Market Outcomes in Low-Income Countries: Methodology

The Supply Side (demand for education)

Economic literature has made considerable progress in identifying the difficulties related to and involved in devising the remedies for consistent estimation of monetary returns to education (Card 1999, 2001; Angrist and Krueger 1999; Blundell, Dearden, and Sianesi 2005). In simplest terms, the rates of return to education are computed by either the cost-benefit method or the Mincerian regression method. The Mincerian regression model is discussed here in detail because it is the most commonly used approach in the literature. (See box 1A.1 for a discussion of problems with estimating income.)

Mincerian Earnings Function Method

This method requires cross-section data on a sample of workers of varying ages and education levels. It is a commonly used approach because it allows for flexible ways of controlling for other worker characteristics and involves estimating a regression in which the log of earnings is the dependent variable and years of schooling, along with other relevant characteristics of the individual, are the explanatory variables. The general form of earnings equation is usually defined as:

$$\ln w_i = \alpha_{ag}\mathbf{x}_i + f_{ag}(s_i) + v_i \tag{1}$$

where w_i is real earnings of individual i, $\mathbf{x}_i$ is a set of worker characteristics excluding education, α_{ag} is a parameter vector, is the years of education, is the earnings-education profile, v_i is a residual, and a and g denote age group and gender, respectively. A very common approach in the literature is to write log earnings as a linear function of years of schooling, and a nonlinear (quadratic) function of years of experience (denoted e)[1]:

$$\ln w_i = \alpha_0 + \alpha_1 e_i + \alpha_2 e_i^2 + rs_i + v_i \tag{2}$$

Jacob Mincer (1974) showed that the coefficient r on years of schooling in such an earnings function is interpretable as the rate of return on education.[2] Early on in the literature, the residual was commonly assumed to be uncorrelated with education and experience, which justified estimating the coefficients using ordinary least squares (OLS). With such an approach, returns to education are usually between 5 and 15 percent, although there are plenty of exceptions to this "rule." The following results, taken from previous research, are illustrative and quite representative:[3]

United States 1973: $\ln w = 6.20 + 0.11s + 0.08e - 0.0012e^2$ ($R^2 = 0.285$)
South Africa 1993: $\ln w = 4.66 + 0.16s + 0.06e - 0.0008e^2$ ($R^2 = 0.316$)
India 1995: $\ln w = 4.70 + 0.11s + 0.07e - 0.0011e^2$ ($R^2 = 0.520$)

The three Mincerian earnings functions thus indicate that the marginal returns to education in the years shown were 11 percent in the United States, 16 percent in South Africa, and 11 percent in India.

The above model is in its simplest form. The two major sources of bias in the OLS estimate of the effect of education on earnings are sample selectivity bias and endogeneity (omitted variable) bias. Sample selectivity bias arises from estimating the earnings function on separate subsamples of workers, each of which may not be a random draw from the population. The problem, in its simpler form, is that individuals differ in the marginal costs incurred or returns to one extra year of education (or both). Hence, inferring from the behavior of one individual with a certain level of education what an individual at random in the population would earn were he or she to achieve this specific education level is likely to lead to erroneous conclusions. In practice, an estimate of the true causal effect of education requires identification of an appropriate counterfactual (what individual i would have earned had that level of education not been achieved) and a comparison of this counterfactual amount with the actual earnings of individual i. Because the model predicts (and data in general confirm) that education is not allocated at random in the population, identifying an appropriate counterfactual is a daunting task—OLS estimates of the returns to education hence are likely to be biased. In particular, if individuals with lower marginal costs of education (for example, because they are not credit constrained) also have higher levels of earnings, irrespective of their level of education, then simple OLS estimates of the returns to education are likely to be upward biased.[4]

Endogeneity bias arises if workers' unobserved traits, which are in the error term, are systematically correlated both with included independent variables and with the dependent variable (earnings). For instance, if worker ability is positively correlated with both education and earnings, then any positive coefficient on education in the earnings function may simply reflect the cross-section correlation between ability on the one hand and both education and earnings on the other, rather than representing a causal effect from education onto earnings.

Four remedies have been devised in the literature to consistently estimate the returns to education.

1. The first approach is to *control for observable characteristics.* Consistency of the estimates requires that conditional on these observables, schooling is randomly allocated. It is likely that the researcher does not have enough information available to measure all the determinants of schooling choices and, most important, the conditional independence assumption is ultimately un-testable. Additionally, it is known that controlling for endogenous variables in the regression might actually lead to inconsistent OLS estimates of the included exogenous variables (Angrist and Krueger 1999).

One variant of this approach is still to control for observables, but in a nonparametric way. The alternative method in this case is *matching* on observables or on *propensity score*, that is, effectively comparing individuals with similar probabilities of receiving treatment, in this case, acquiring a certain level of education (Angrist and Krueger 1998). This method assumes that assignment to treatment for two individuals with equal probability of receiving treatment is random. Although this method warrants more flexibility than the one that controls parametrically on observables, it has its own drawbacks (most important, treatment and control groups need to have a common support). Ultimately, this method is again based on an assumption (conditional independence of treatment and outcome) that is hard to hold (except in special cases) and ultimately untestable. The literature has many examples of this type of approach, for instance, Blundell, Dearden, and Sianesi (2005) present matching estimates for the United Kingdom.

2. A second approach relies on *first differences between siblings and twins.* The idea is that twins (and to some extent, siblings) share the same genetics and family background. If one is willing to assume that differences in their education are purely random (that is, uncorrelated with unobservable determinants of earnings, perhaps conditional on some observed factors such as order of birth and gender), then differences in their earnings should only reflect differences in their education. By differentiating across siblings, in practice, one filters out all potential correlation between education and unobserved determinants of earnings that are common to all siblings in the household. One can simply run an OLS regression of differences in earnings on differences in education across siblings or twins (a family fixed effect model) to consistently estimate the returns to education. There are different examples of this type of regression in the literature (for instance, Ashenfelter and Zimmermann 1997; Ashenfelter and Krueger 1994; Ashenfelter and Rouse 1998; and Hertz 2003) that propose more sophisticated variants of this approach.

3. A third and more promising approach relies on *instrumental variables (IV).* The idea of this approach is to exploit only the variation in schooling that is uncorrelated with unobserved determinants of earnings. Because individuals equalize marginal returns to marginal costs, in order to consistently identify the (marginal) return schedule, one needs some variation on the side of costs. Typically, researchers have used instruments such as construction of schools, distance to school, compulsory schooling, or child labor laws (Card 1995; Duflo 2001; Moretti 2004 a, 2004b; Acemoglu and Angrist 2000). All these policy instruments tend to affect enrollment.

Instrumental variables estimates suffer from some weaknesses, too. First, unless the model is overidentified, the exclusion restriction cannot be tested. Second, when returns to education are heterogeneous, one is likely to identify the effect only among compliers, that is, the ones who (assuming monotonic compliance) change their behavior because of the policy instrument (Angrist and Krueger 1998). This is a localized effect that might reflect the behavior of specific groups of individuals. Hence, inferring from the IV estimates the causal effect of one extra year of education in the population at large might be misleading.

A variant of the IV model is the *control function (CF)* approach (also known as the Heckman correction method). Rather than only using the exogenous variation in schooling to identify the effect of interest, this approach explicitly controls for the selection term in the wage equation. The consistency of the CF estimator is also based on some exclusion restrictions (as in the IV approach), in addition to a parametric assumption on the distribution of the unobservable responsible for the endogeneity (Flabbi, Paternostro, and Tiongson 2007).[5]

4. A fourth approach that has been used with some success and is increasingly popular is based on *regression discontinuity (RD)* (Oreopoulos 2006). If one is able to identify a discontinuous jump in the schooling variable (possibly induced by a sharp policy change), one can attempt to identify the effect of education on wages by examining the behavior of wages in the neighborhood of this discontinuity point. For education to have a positive effect on earnings, in fact, one would expect a positive discrete jump in earnings around this same point. This approach, which is effectively a localized difference-in-difference, requires fewer assumptions than other approaches (Hahn, Todd, and Klaauw 2002). A fundamental identification assumption is that the latent distribution of earnings is continuous in schooling. This also rules out potential endogenous sorting around the discontinuity point.

Certain caveats in the recommended remedies. The suitability of the different approaches outlined (rather simply) above depends very much on the problem at hand and available data. Although in general, one can, in most data sets, implement strategies based on controls on observables or even matching, this does not seem a very promising estimation strategy, unless one has good reasons to believe that all the variables that determine selection into a certain education level are available and accounted for.

The first differences between siblings and twins approach has its own problems because it is known that first differences (between twins or siblings) potentially exacerbate measurement error. Additional difficulties arise from the fact that these estimates are hard to extrapolate to the population at large. With regard to data requirements, differences between twins or siblings require having information on the level of education of siblings by the time they are adults. This approach thus requires data different from typical household survey data, because in general, siblings are not observed in household surveys unless they cohabit (hence, representing a much-selected sample).

The IV approach is widely used in the literature. However, it requires having a suitable instrument for education. Typically, major policy changes appear as potential avenues, although these are commonly thought to have general equilibrium effects that are often ignored (one exception being Duflo [2004]). One advantage of IV estimates is that they often also allow controlling for omitted variable bias. However, IV approaches lead to erroneous conclusions if the instrument is not excludable from the earnings equation (a classical example of this being parental education, which is likely to affect children's earnings for reasons other than its effect on wages). If the model is overidentified, there is a way to test for the internal consistency of the instruments. One should, though, stay away from models with too many instruments because it is well known that the IV estimates tend to be biased toward the OLS estimates (Staiger and Stock 1997).

The regression discontinuity (either fuzzy or sharp) approach is essentially the most promising one. However, this approach—perhaps more than the others—is very problem dependent. There is no guarantee that such discontinuities arise in practice in the data and one needs a large mass of data around the discontinuity for identification.

Accounting for heterogeneity in ability. The OLS regression is based on the mean of the conditional earnings distribution. This approach assumes that possible differences in the impacts of the exogenous variables along the conditional distribution are unimportant. However, if schooling affects the conditional distribution of the dependent variable differently at different points in the wage distribution, then quantile regressions (QR) are useful because they allow the contribution of schooling to vary along the distribution of the dependent variable. Using quantile regressions, one can investigate how wages vary with education at the 25th (low), 50th (median), and 75th (high) percentiles of the distribution of earnings.

To the extent that one is willing to interpret observations close to the 75th percentile as indicative of higher "ability" (on the grounds that such observations have atypically high wages, given their socio-demographic characteristics), quantile regressions are indicative of the effect of education on earnings across individuals with varying ability. However, this holds if one assumes that education is exogenous, which is not a valid a priori assumption. Thus, one cannot say that the return to education for, say, the 90th percentile gives the true return to education for high-ability people, purged of ability bias. The same caution is given in Arias, Hallock, and Sosa-Escudero (2001), who cite QR studies of returns to education (Buchinsky 1994; Machado and Mata 2000; Mwabu and Schultz 1996) and say that the results of these studies should be interpreted with caution because they do not handle the problems of endogeneity bias.

Analyzing the Demand Side

The demand for labor is a derived demand, with two dimensions for policy. The first is the types of jobs that are created as demand expands. Such an approach sees the policy issues as arising in markets other than the labor market. The second considers possible policy problems in the operations of the labor market. This approach focuses on supply-side issues, which include the match between the supply and demand for skills, the link between the wages paid by a firm or employer and its productivity, and the role of labor market regulation in limiting the willingness of firms to hire. The two approaches are complementary and directly linked.

An analysis of the first dimension requires that the types of jobs that have been created in an economy be examined, and the way in which these are linked to the expansion (or contraction) of the economy. This analysis can use the sectoral breakdown from a multitopic household survey, such as the Living Standards Measurement Survey, or a labor force survey. Repeated cross-sections can be used to shed light on the shift in relative demand for education over a period of time by analyzing the changes in relative supply of workers with different education levels and the relative returns to these levels (see Katz and Murphy [1992] for a detailed methodology).

Within these sectors, what factors affect labor demand? This is the second dimension to determining labor demand. Supply-side factors, which include wages and skills, will determine which firms form and which grow. It is not simply the number of jobs that is important to policy makers; it is the type of jobs. This issue needs a different kind of information base, one ideally provided by firm-level surveys. Firm-level surveys have not been common in low-income countries. However, the development of Investment Climate Assessment surveys since the late

1990s has provided the much-needed information for many countries. Unfortunately, the education modules in these surveys are generally not well developed (with notable exceptions), but still give some insight into the effective demand for the type of education and skills in firms (see, for instance, Lukyanova et al. [2007]; Riboud, Savchenko, and Tan [2007]; Batra and Stone [2004]).[6]

Based on the policy issues identified above, a comprehensive picture of the demand side for skills and education in the labor markets requires that the following issues be examined, based on a combination of data sources, such as multitopic household surveys, labor force surveys, firm-level surveys, and information from relevant ministries in a given country:

- *Formal and informal job creation.* Depending on the country context, identification of the sources of job creation is critical (for example, informal versus formal sector, public versus private sector, and so forth).
- *Education and earnings in formal and informal jobs.* The creation and destruction of jobs in various sectors have important repercussions for the types of education and skill sets demanded in the labor market. In Ghana, for instance, the public sector and large firms exhibited the greatest demand for skills related to formal education and experience acquired on the job. So the changing pattern of labor demand suggests a decrease in the demand for skilled workers.
- *Labor regulations and unionization in the dominant employment sectors.* Hiring and firing rules in the dominant employment sectors must be understood (for instance, whether employment guarantees are in place for certain occupations), as must minimum wage laws, employee protection regulations, and taxation. Unionization of the labor force and the dynamics of negotiations between employers and unions can be critical in determining labor market outcomes and even the value of particular skills and education.
- *The macroeconomic context.* Last, it is extremely important to take into account the overall macroeconomic context, because jobs, particularly good jobs, are dependent on a number of enabling factors, including the investment climate, capital flows, and financial markets. The prices of raw materials for the manufacturing sector, the exchange rate for the trading industry, the policies on FDI, as well as the level of technological advancement, will all determine how many workers and which skill sets are demanded in the labor markets.

Tracer studies that follow cohorts of education graduates in the labor markets over time are useful in exploring these issues. Such studies, although usually conducted on a smaller scale (because of the expense), give much better insight into the actual labor market outcomes for individuals over time.

The potential for a detailed analysis of the demand side is vast. With the increasing availability of various types of data sets for a number of low-income countries, a comprehensive analysis of the demand for skills and education can be conducted, within the country context and focusing on the relevant indicators.

Box 1A.1

The outcome variable: Estimating the income variable

A problem that arises in estimating the returns to education in many low- and middle-income countries involves the outcome variables. Typically, wage equations present weekly or hourly wages as a dependent variable. These regressions refer typically only to employees. Because unemployment and nonparticipation are not major issues (at least for men, and at least in developed countries), potential selection issues are often ignored in the research literature (although selection into self-employment cannot and has not been ignored). The problem gets complicated in countries such as the Arab Republic of Egypt, Ghana, and Pakistan where a nonnegligible share of the population is out of work, either because of unemployment or nonparticipation. Thus, the econometric issue is that individuals in employment might not be a random sample of the population. Theory predicts that only individuals with market wages above the reservation wage (or their farm productivity) are employed. This implies that the wage profiles among those currently in work might not be a good indicator of what an individual at random in the population would make were she or he to be employed. One approach is to include a selection term in the wage equation for employment. This requires finding an instrument for participation that is uncorrelated with market wages. One such instrument for women is number of children, which is thought to affect the reservation wage but not the market wage. A comparable instrument for men is harder to find.

(continued)

Box 1A.1

(Continued)

An alternative approach consists in controlling nonparametrically for selection. A number of papers now propose easy-to-implement procedures to control for selection, and obtain either consistent estimates of the conditional median (Chandra 2003; Olivetti and Petrongolo 2005) or bounds around this (Lee 2005). The idea of the first approach to controlling nonparametrically for selection is to re-impute individuals with no wages. If one is willing to make assumptions (perhaps supported by observable characteristics in the data) on where the nonemployed individuals come from in the distribution of market wages (that is, below or above the median of their group), then one can recover consistent estimates of the conditional median of these groups (provided selection is below 50 percent). Under symmetry, this is identical to the conditional mean. The second approach—the trimming approach—requires instead imposing the same percentage of selection in the treatment and control groups by artificially dropping (as opposed to imputing back) some observations. Unless one has some strong prior information on where selected individuals come from (whether from the top or bottom of the distribution), one can derive best and worst case scenario estimates of the conditional mean assuming opposite (that is, perfect positive or perfect negative) selection. This gives upper and lower bounds estimates for the true effect. These procedures are easy to implement and require no exclusion restriction. They require, though, strong assumptions on the direction of selection (in the case of re-imputation) and might not be very informative (in the case of bounds) when selection is large and, hence, bounds are far apart.

Sources: Kingdon and Soderbom 2007a, 2007b; Manacorda 2007.

Notes

1. Age-earnings profiles typically show that earnings increase with experience, but at a decreasing rate; this provides the basis for the inclusion of both experience and its square.

2. Strictly speaking, the coefficient on s is simply the marginal benefit and not the marginal return to schooling, because it does not take into account the direct costs of education (for an advanced discussion, see Heckman, Lochner, and Todd [2006]). Private returns to education are always higher than the social returns if education is publicly subsidized.

3. The U.S. equation is taken from Mincer (1974) and those for South Africa and India are taken from Kingdon and Knight (2004) and Kingdon (1998), respectively.

4. However, if individuals have different marginal returns to education, and—as appears plausible—individuals with higher marginal costs also have higher marginal returns (and lower schooling), the bias might be in the opposite direction.

5. For a technical discussion, see Heckman (1979).

6. The drawback of using most firm-level surveys is the limited size and scope of the surveys. Some are limited to only small and medium enterprises, others to a few hundred of the thousands of enterprises in a country. In addition, most do not cover the informal or unregistered enterprises that employ the most vulnerable members of the population.

Data and Methodology for Pakistan and Ghana Case Studies

Population and Data

The empirical work on the country case studies was based mainly on large datasets created from household surveys in Ghana (the Ghana Living Standards Survey for 1998/99) and Pakistan (Pakistan Integrated Household Surveys 1998/99 and 2001/02). These surveys are broadly representative of the population of households in these countries. The vast majority of earnings regressions in the literature, both on developed and developing countries, were estimated based on samples of wage employees only. This is reasonable for studies for developed countries, where large proportions of the workforce are indeed wage employees. In developing countries, however, wage employment is typically a small and often shrinking part of the labor market (Johanson and Adams 2004; Teal, Sandefur, and Monk 2007).

Studies that attempt to document the relationships between skills and labor market outcomes in poor countries might be incomplete if they focus solely on wage employment. Indeed, in the data from Ghana, only 12 percent of the individuals surveyed were wage employees, while in the Pakistan data, between 25 and 27 percent of the surveyed individuals had a wage job. In view of this fact, the investigation focuses on the connections between education and labor market outcomes across five broadly defined occupational categories: the wage employed, the nonfarm self-employed, farmers and agricultural workers, the unemployed, and people who are out of the labor force (not seeking work). Clearly, the labor market benefits of education and skills accrue both from education promoting a person's entry into the lucrative occupations and, conditional on occupation, by raising earnings. Typically, for example, earnings in formal wage employment are significantly higher than in agriculture. Therefore, in the case studies, the relationship between education and skills and occupational outcomes were carefully analyzed. Specifically, multinomial logits were estimated in which occupational attainment was modeled as a function of education or skills, plus a range of control variables.

Explanatory Variables in Earnings Regressions

The primary objective of the analysis was to estimate the total returns to education; explanatory variables were selected accordingly. In particular, in estimating the earnings regressions, variables that are determined by education are not conditioned because such conditioning would change the interpretation of the schooling effects. For example, it is likely that important effects of education include enabling individuals to get high-wage jobs (for example, managerial positions); enabling them to get into certain high-wage sectors or firms; and generating job security and thus work experience. Consequently, occupation, firm-level variables, work experience, and other variables sometimes seen on the right-hand side in earnings regressions were not conditioned. The preferred specifications for the earnings regressions also did not condition land in the agricultural earnings equation, or capital stock for the self-employed, because investment in these assets may be driven by education. (A brief discussion of the effects of including these additional control variables on the results can be found later in this appendix). The preferred specifications thus included only a small set of control variables, with age and gender emphasized the most. Controls for province fixed effects were also included.

Analytical Approach

It is widely believed that education affects people's economic status by raising their earnings in the labor market. However, education may raise earnings through a number of different channels, such as improving access to employment or, conditional on employment, promoting entry into higher-paying occupations or industries. In the country case studies, both the total effect of education on earnings and the role of education in occupational attainment were explored, because the latter is an important mechanism through which the market benefits of education are realized. The earnings function for wage employees is specified in general form as:

$$\ln w_i = \alpha_{ag}\mathbf{x}_i + f_{ag}(s_i) + v_i \tag{1}$$

where w_i is real earnings of individual i, $\mathbf{x}_i$ is a vector of worker characteristics excluding education, α_{ag} is a parameter vector, s_i is the years of education, $f_{ag}(\cdot)$ is the earnings-education profile, v_i is a residual, and a and g denote age group and gender, respectively. The primary objective of the background papers was to estimate the total returns to education, and the variables included in the $\mathbf{x}_i$ were selected accordingly.

Estimation of the earnings-education profile $f_{ag}(.)$ was critical to the analysis, which focused on two specifications: a standard linear model and a model with dummy variables for highest level of education completed. The former is attractive partly because the results are straightforward to interpret, whereas the latter is an attractive way of analyzing how returns to education differ across different levels of education. In addition, another model was considered in which a quadratic term was added to the linear specification—a convenient way of testing for nonlinearities in the earnings-education profile.

In the empirical analysis, earnings regressions were estimated based on data from three labor market subsectors: wage employment, self-employment, and agriculture. Among the wage employed, individual data on earnings as well as on the explanatory variables were available. For individuals who were either self-employed or worked in the agricultural sector, no earnings data existed at the individual level. Instead, earnings at the household level were available, distinguishing between earnings for self-employed and earnings for agricultural workers. To identify the parameters in the earnings function (1), the explanatory variables need to be aggregated so that they are defined at the same level of aggregation as the dependent variable. Thus, for agriculture and self-employment, the estimable earnings equation is written

$$\ln \overline{w}_{hc} = \alpha_{at}\overline{\mathbf{x}}_{hc} + \overline{[f_{at}\,(s_i)]}_{hc} + \overline{\upsilon}_{hc} \tag{1}$$

where hc are household-category subscripts, and the bar-superscript indicates household-category averages.

Endogeneity Bias

The two major sources of bias in the ordinary least squares (OLS) estimate of the effect of education on earnings are sample selectivity bias and endogeneity (omitted variable) bias. Sample selectivity bias arises as a result of estimating the earnings function from separate subsamples of workers, each of which may not be a random draw from the population. This process violates a fundamental assumption of the least squares regression model. While modeling occupational outcomes is a useful exercise in its own right—suggesting the way in which education influences people's decision to participate in wage, self-, or agricultural employment—it is also needed for consistent estimation of earnings functions. Modeling participation in different occupations is the first step of the Heckman procedure to correct for sample selectivity: probabilities predicted by the occupational choice model are used to derive the selectivity term that is used in the earnings function.

Adding a subscript j to denote occupation type to the earnings function (1),

$$\ln w_{ij} = \alpha_{ag\,j}\mathbf{x}_{ij} + f_{agi}\,(s_{ij}) + \upsilon_{ij} \tag{1'}$$

it follows that the expected value of the dependent variable, conditional on the explanatory variables x and s, and selection into occupation j, is equal to

$$E(\ln w_{ij}|\,\mathbf{x}_{ij},\,s_{ij},\,m_{ij} = 1)\;\alpha_{ag\,j}\mathbf{x}_{ij} + f_{agi}\,(s_{ij}) + E(\upsilon_{ij}|m_{ij} = 1) \tag{2}$$

where m_{ij} is a dummy variable equal to one if occupation j was selected and zero otherwise. The last term in (2) is not necessarily equal to zero in the sample of observations in sector j, in which case estimating the wage equation ignoring sample selection will lead to biased estimates. For example, if more highly motivated or more ambitious people systematically select into particular occupations—for example, into waged work—then people in the waged subsample would, on average, be more motivated and ambitious than those in the rest of the population.

Thus, $E(v_{ij}|m_{ij}= 1)$ is not zero in this subsample because the waged workers' subsample is not a random draw from the whole population. Least squares would therefore yield inconsistent parameter estimates. Following Heckman (1979) and Lee (1983), the earnings equations can be corrected for selectivity by including the inverse of Mills' ratio λ_{ji} as an additional explanatory variable in the wage equation, so that

$$\ln w_{ij} = \alpha_{agj}\mathbf{x}_{ij} + f_{agj}\left(s_{ij}\right) + \theta_{agj}\lambda_{ij}\left(z_{ij}\gamma\right) + \varepsilon_{ij}, \tag{2}$$

where z_{ij} is a set of variables explaining selection into occupation and γ are the associated coefficients. Thus, the probability of selection into each occupation type is first estimated by fitting a model of occupational attainment, based on which the selectivity term (λ) is computed.[1] The coefficients on the lambda terms λ_j will be a measure of the bias from nonrandom sample selection. If these are statistically different from zero, the null hypothesis of "no bias" is rejected.

Another issue is "endogeneity" or omitted variable bias. The analysis attempted to address the problem of endogeneity by estimating a family fixed effects regression on earnings. To the extent that unobserved traits are shared within the family, their effect will be netted out in a family differenced model. For instance, the error term "difference in ability between members" will be zero if ability is equal among members. While it is unlikely that unobserved traits are identical across family members, it is likely that they are much more similar within a family than across families and, as such, family fixed effects estimation gives an estimate of the return to education that reduces endogeneity bias without necessarily eliminating it entirely.

Note

1. The inverse Mills' ratio is defined as $\lambda_{ji} = \dfrac{\phi(H_{ij})}{\Phi(H_{ij})}$, where $H_{ij} = \Phi^{-1}(P_{ij})$, $\phi(\cdot)$ is the standard normal density function, $\Phi(\cdot)$ the normal distribution function, and P_{ij} is the estimated probability that the ith worker chooses the jth occupation.

Summary of Empirical Literature on the Effect of Basic Cognitive Skills on Earnings

Low-income countries and International Development Association (IDA) borrowers

Study and objective	Model and method	Data	Main results
Ghana			
"Skills, Schooling, and Household Income in Ghana" (Jolliffe 1998) *Objective:* Estimate the effect of cognitive skills on the incomes of Ghanaian households.	Three reduced-form income functions. Scores on mathematics and English tests are used as measures of cognitive skills, and the returns to these skills are measured by estimating farm profit, off-farm income, and total income.	Ghana Living Standards Survey, 1988–89	Test scores are important determinants of total income and off-farm income. They do not appear to be important determinants of farm income. Main findings show that an increase of one standard deviation from household average scores results in an increase in total income of 9.6 percent.

(continued)

Low-income countries and International Development Association (IDA) borrowers (continued)

Study and objective	Model and method	Data	Main results
Kenya and Tanzania			
"Earnings, Schooling, Ability, and Cognitive Skills" (Boissiere, Knight, and Sabot 1985) *Objective:* Attempt to distinguish the influence on earnings of cognitive achievement, native ability, and years of education as a means of adjudicating the human capital, screening, and credentialist hypotheses.	Conventional earnings functions.	Comparable surveys administered by the authors in Kenya and Tanzania in 1980.	Estimates from conventional earnings functions indicate that in Kenya, secondary leavers are paid 61 percent more than primary leavers. The figure for Tanzania is 32 percent. Returns to reasoning ability in the labor market are small; those to years of education are moderate; and those to literacy and numeracy are large. The schooling coefficient fell by two-thirds upon the introduction of a cognitive skill variable, but remained statistically significant.
Pakistan			
"School Quality and Cognitive Achievement Production: A Case Study for Rural Pakistan" (Behrman et al. 1997) *Objective:* Examine the importance of school inputs in rural Pakistan.	Production functions for cognitive achievement as measured by tests of literacy and numeracy. The major direct determinants of cognitive achievement are classified as years of schooling, school quality, parental inputs into the learning process, and the individual's potential to learn.	Multipurpose survey panel of 800 households collected by the International Food Policy Research Institute in 1989 and results from tests of literacy and numeracy designed by the Educational Testing Service.	A 10 percent increase in schooling attainment raises reading and math scores by just over 4 percent. A 10 percent increase in teacher quality indexes raises predicted reading test score by 3 percent and math score by 2 percent. Lowering the student-teacher ratio by 10 percent raises predicted math score by 2 percent and, treating the coefficient as a best estimate, predicted reading score by 1 percent.

Study and objective	Model and method	Data	Main results
Pakistan			
"Decomposing the Gender Gap in Cognitive Skills in a Poor Rural Economy" (Alderman et al. 1996) *Objective:* Investigate the determinants of the educational gender gap in rural Pakistan.	Reduced-form demand relations for starting school and for cognitive achievement.	Multipurpose survey panel of 800 households collected by the International Food Policy Research Institute in 1989 and results from tests of literacy and numeracy designed by the Educational Testing Service.	Gender gaps in school enrollments and in cognitive achievement are large in rural Pakistan. The findings suggest that a large portion of these gaps are due to gender differences in local school availability. Solely by eliminating the gender gap in local primary school availability, the gender gap in total cognitive achievement for the cohort ages 10–25 could have been reduced almost a third and that in literacy by over 40 percent.
Colombia			
"Schooling, Ability, and Earnings in Colombia, 1988" (Psacharopoulos and Velez 1992) *Objective:* Explore the earnings-education-ability nexus.	Standard human capital equation plus reasoning and cognitive ability variables.	Sample of 2,100 workers collected in 1988. Cognitive achievement was assessed using items designed to evaluate general knowledge not exclusively related to the content of formal education.	The return to education in the conventional model is 10 percent. When adding ability alone, it drops to 9.4 percent. When cognitive knowledge is entered, the return falls to 8.9 percent, which is expected given the high correlation between years of schooling and cognitive knowledge.

(continued)

Low-income countries and International Development Association (IDA) borrowers (continued)

Study and objective	Model and method	Data	Main results
Morocco			
"The Effect of a Change in Language of Instruction on the Returns to Schooling in Morocco" (Angrist and Lavy 1997) *Objective:* Analyze how a policy change (language instruction for new cohorts of Moroccan sixth graders switches from French to Arabic) affected the French language skills on test scores and earnings.	Conventional earnings functions estimated by ordinary least squares (OLS) and two-stage least squares (2SLS).	Moroccan Labor Force Surveys of 1990 and 1991 and the 1991 Living Standard Measurement and Literacy Survey.	Arabization program reduced middle school wage premium by 27 percent and 19 percent for weekly and monthly wages, respectively. OLS estimates between language skills and earnings suggest that going from minimal skills to functional competence in written French raises earnings by about 17 percent. 2SLS estimates of effect of test scores on earnings indicate that going from some ability to functional competence raises earnings by more than 50 percent.
South Africa			
"Does School Quality Matter? Returns to Education and the Characteristics of Schools in South Africa" (Case and Yogo 1999) *Objective:* Estimate the effects of school quality—measured by the pupil/teacher ratio—and contribute to what is known about the impact of school quality, by documenting its effect on the incomes of Black South Africans.	Conventional linear relationship between schooling and earnings and a second step estimation.	South African census and two national surveys of school quality (1996).	A decrease in the pupil/teacher ratio of 5 students would, on average, be associated with an increase in the return to education of roughly 1 percent. In terms of the effect of school quality on educational attainment, reducing the pupil/teacher ratio by 10 students would, all else equal, increase completed schooling by 0.6 years.

Study and objective	Model and method	Data	Main results
South Africa			
"Primary Schooling, Cognitive Skills, and Wages in South Africa" (Moll 1998) *Objective:* Test the hypothesis that the education offered to blacks in South Africa was of no use to the market, by examining whether the African schooling system generated cognitive skills, and whether these skills were rewarded by employers.	Conventional earnings functions specification with cognitive skills as independent variable. Instrumental variables.	Project for Statistics on Living Standards and Development (1993).	Each extra point on the cognitive achievement score raises wages by 10 percent. When splitting the total score into its comprehension and computational components, only the latter is significant (0.21 percent in the case of OLS), while the coefficient on comprehension is small and insignificant. The robust estimation techniques and instrumental variables estimation do not qualitatively alter the conclusion drawn from the OLS estimates.
Canada			
"Minorities, Cognitive Skills and Incomes of Canadians" (Finnie and Meng 2001) *Objective:* Investigate the role of literacy and numeracy as determinants of labor market outcomes.	Standard human capital equation plus literacy and numeracy variables.	Statistics Canada's Survey of Literacy Skills Used in Daily Activities (1989).	OLS estimates for the log annual income conventional equation show that the inclusion of numeracy affects male income levels (1.07) and the inclusion of literacy has little influence. For females the reverse is true. The inclusion of literacy affects female income levels (2.14) and the inclusion of numeracy has little influence.

(continued)

Low-income countries and International Development Association (IDA) borrowers (continued)

Study and objective	Model and method	Data	Main results
Canada			
"Literacy, Numeracy and Labor Market Outcomes" (Green and Riddell 2001) *Objective:* Analyze the role of observed skills—specifically, prose, document, and quantitative literacy—on individual labor market earnings.	Amended human capital earnings function to deal with the situation of observable and unobservable skills.	Canadian data from the 1994 International Adult Literacy Survey.	The conventional rate of return for education is 8.3 percent and observed skills have a large and statistically significant causal effect on earnings: an increase of 10 points on the literacy scale raises earnings by 3.1 percent. The inclusion of the literacy score variable reduces the estimated coefficient from 8.3 percent to 5.2 percent, suggesting that one-third of the return may be due to the combined effects of education in observed skills and of observed skills on earnings.
United Kingdom			
"Measuring and Assessing the Impact of Basic Skills on Labor Market Outcomes" (McIntosh and Vignoles 2001) *Objective:* Evaluate the impact of numeracy and literacy skills on workers' labor market outcomes.	Conventional earnings functions.	National Child Development Study and the International Adult Literacy Survey (1995).	Individuals with level 1 numeracy skills earn 11–12 percent more than individuals below that numeracy level. The wage premium associated with level 1 literacy skills is only slightly smaller than the numeracy effect. Results are consistent in both data sets. Women seem to earn a higher premium for having better numeracy and literacy skills than men.

Study and objective	Model and method	Data	Main results
United States			
"Cognitive Ability and the Rising Return to Education" (Cawley, Heckman, and Vytlacil 1998) *Objective:* Examine the contribution of the rise of return to ability to the rise in the economic return to education following a small range of birth cohorts over time.	The structure of the data creates an identification problem that makes it impossible to identify main age and time effects and to isolate all possible age-time interactions. This problem is solved using nonparametric methods: estimation of time effects within education-ability-age groups for white males.	National Longitudinal Survey of Youth (1979–94).	There is little evidence that the rise in the return to education is generated by a rise in the return to ability.
"Using Siblings to Estimate the Effect of School Quality on Wages" (Altonji and Dunn 1996b) *Objective:* Estimate the effects of school inputs on wages using the variance across siblings and school characteristics.	Conventional earnings functions specification. Instrumental variables.	National Longitudinal Surveys of Labor Market Experience of Young Men and Young Women (1988).	Increases in teachers' salary and expenditures per pupil leads to wage increases of 10.6 percent and 5.6 percent, respectively, for a student who leaves school after high school. Similar results were obtained when using an instrumental variables fixed effects scheme to deal with possible endogeneity of variation across siblings in school quality.

(continued)

Low-income countries and International Development Association (IDA) borrowers (continued)

Study and objective	Model and method	Data	Main results
United States			
"How Important Are the Cognitive Skills of Teenagers in Predicting Subsequent Earnings?" (Murnane et al. 2000) *Objective:* Examine whether basic cognitive skills (as distinct from formal schooling) influence wage determination.	Conventional earnings functions with natural logarithm of hourly wages "x" years after graduation from high school.	National Longitudinal Study of High School Class of 1972 (NLS72) and High School and Beyond of 1991 (HS&B).	Coefficient on math score for the NLS72 males indicates that a one-point difference in the math score of male high school seniors in 1972 is associated with a 2 percent difference in annual earnings at age 31. For the coefficient on math score for HS&B males, a one-point difference in the math score of male high school seniors in 1982 is associated with a 1.5 percent difference in annual earnings at age 27.
"Does School Quality Matter? Evidence from the National Longitudinal Survey of Youth" (Betts 1995) *Objective:* Search for links between school quality and subsequent earnings of students.	Tests for the relationship between the log weekly wage of white males and the quality of the high school attended by individuals.	National Longitudinal Survey of Youth (1979–90).	Earnings of white male workers depend significantly on which high school they attended. Standard benchmarks of school quality (teacher-pupil ratio, the relative salary of starting teachers, and the percentage of teachers with Master's degrees or higher) explain very little of these differences between schools.

Study and objective	Model and method	Data	Main results
United States			
"Does School Quality Matter? Returns to Education and the Characteristics of Public Schools in the United States" (Card and Krueger 1992) *Objective:* Estimate the effects of school quality—measured by the pupil/teacher ratio, average term length, and relative teacher pay—on the rate of return to education for men born between 1920 and 1949.	Conventional linear relationship between schooling and earnings and a second step estimation.	United States Census (1980).	Coefficients of the three measures of school quality suggest a quantitatively important effect on the return to education. A decrease in the pupil/teacher ratio by 10 students raises average earnings by 4.2 percent and a 30 percent increase in teachers' wages increases average log wages by 1.3 percent.

References and Other Resources

Acemoglu, D. 2002. "Technological Change, Inequality, and the Labor Market." *Journal of Economic Literature* 40 (1): 7–72.

Acemoglu, Daron, and Joshua Angrist. 2000. "How Large are Human-Capital Externalities? Evidence from Compulsory-Schooling Laws." In *NBER Macroeconomics Annual 2000*, ed. Ben S. Bernanke and Kenneth Rogoff, 9–58. MIT Press: Cambridge, MA.

Adams J., M. Greig, and R. W. McQuaid. 2000. "Mismatch Unemployment and Local Labour-Market Efficiency: The Role of Employer and Vacancy Characteristics." *Environment and Planning* 32 (10): 1841–56.

AFESD (Arab Fund for Economic and Social Development). 2003. "The Mismatch Between Educational Achievement and the Arab Labor Market with a Gender Perspective." In *Arab Women in Economic Development*, ed. Heba Handoussa. Cairo.

Alderman, Harold, Jere R. Behrman, Shahrukh Khan, David Ross, and Richard Sabot. 1997. "The Income Gap in Cognitive Skills in Rural Pakistan." *Economic Development and Cultural Change* 46 (1): 97–122.

Alderman, Harold, Jere R. Behrman, David Ross, and Richard Sabot. 1996. "Decomposing the Gender Gap in Cognitive Skills in a Poor Rural Economy." *Journal of Human Resources* 31(1): 229–54.

Alderman, Harold, Peter F. Orazem, and Elizabeth M. Paterno. 2001. "School Quality, School Cost, and the Public/Private School Choices of Low-Income Households in Pakistan." *Journal of Human Resources* 36 (2): 304–26.

Alofs, M. 2002. "Migration Probability as an Incentive for Human Capital Accumulation when Information is Asymmetric." Working Paper, Faculty of Applied Economics, University of Antwerp, Belgium.

Al-Samarrai, Samer, and Paul Bennell. 2007. "Where Has All the Education Gone in Sub-Saharan Africa? Employment and Other Outcomes among Secondary School and University Leavers." *Journal of Development Studies* 43 (7): 1270–1300.

Altonji, Joseph G., and Thomas A. Dunn. 1996a. "The Effects of School and Family Characteristics on the Return to Education." *Review of Economics and Statistics* 78 (4): 692–704.

———. 1996b. "Using Siblings to Estimate the Effect of School Quality on Wages." *Review of Economics and Statistics* 78 (4): 665–71.

Altonji, Joseph G., and Charles R. Pierret. 2001. "Employer Learning and Statistical Discrimination." *Quarterly Journal of Economics* 116 (1): 313–50.

Angrist, Joshua, E. Bettinger, and M. Kremer. 2006. "Long-term Educational Consequences of Secondary School Vouchers: Evidence from Administrative Records in Colombia." *American Economic Review* 96 (3): 847–62.

Angrist, Joshua D., and Alan B. Krueger. 1999. "Empirical Strategies in Labor Economics." In *Handbook of Labor Economics*, edition 1, volume 3, ed. O. Ashenfelter and D. Card, 1277–366. Amsterdam: North Holland.

Angrist, Joshua D., and Victor Lavy. 1997. "The Effect of a Change in Language of Instruction on the Returns to Schooling in Morocco." *Journal of Labor Economics* 15: S48–S76.

Arias, O., K. Hallock, and W. Sosa-Escudero. 2001. "Individual Heterogeneity in the Returns to Schooling: Instrumental Variables Quantile Regression Using Twins Data." *Empirical Economics* 26: 7–40.

Arriagada, Ana-Maria, and Adrian Ziderman. 1992. "Vocational Secondary Schooling, Occupational Choice and Earnings in Brazil." Policy Research Working Paper 1037, Population and Human Resources Department, World Bank, Washington, DC.

Ashenfelter, Orley, and Alan B. Krueger. 1994. "Estimates of the Economic Returns to Schooling from a New Sample of Twins." *American Economic Review* 84 (5): 1157–73.

Ashenfelter, Orley, and Cecelia Rouse. 1998. "Income, Schooling, and Ability: Evidence from a New Sample of Identical Twins." *Quarterly Journal of Economics* 113 (1): 253–84.

Ashenfelter, Orley, and David J. Zimmermann. 1997. "Estimates of the Returns to Schooling from Sibling Data: Fathers, Sons, and Brothers." *The Review of Economics and Statistics* 79 (1): 1–9.

Attanasio, Orazio, Adriana Kugler, and Costas Meghir. 2007. "Effects of Youth Training in Developing Countries: Evidence from a Randomized Training Program in Colombia." Unpublished, University College London.

Barrera-Osorio, Felipe. 2007. "The Impact of Private Provision of Public Education: Empirical Evidence from Bogotá's Concession Schools." Policy Research Working Paper No. 4121, World Bank, Washington, DC.

Batra, Geeta, and Andrew H. W. Stone. 2004. "Investment Climate, Capabilities, and Firm Performance: Evidence from the World Business Environment Survey." Investment Climate Department, World Bank, Washington, DC.

Becker, G. 1964. *Human Capital.* New York: National Bureau of Economic Research.

Behrman, Jere R., Shahrukh Khan, David Ross, and Richard Sabot. 1997. "School Quality and Cognitive Achievement Production: A Case Study for Rural Pakistan." *Economics of Education Review* 16 (2): 127–42.

Behrman, Jere R., David Ross, and Richard Sabot. 2002. "Improving the Quality versus Increasing the Quantity of Schooling: Evidence from Rural Pakistan." PIER Working Paper No. 02-022. Penn Institute for Economic Research, Department of Economics, University of Pennsylvania, Philadelphia.

———. 2008. "Improving the Quality Versus Increasing the Quantity of Schooling: Estimates of Rates of Return from Rural Pakistan." *Journal of Development Economics* 85 (1): 94–104.

Betcherman, Gordon, Martin Godfrey, Susana Puerto, Friederike Rother, and Antoneta Stavreska. 2007. "A Review of Interventions to Support Young Workers: Findings of the Youth Employment Inventory." Social Protection Discussion Paper No. 0715, World Bank, Washington, DC.

Betcherman, Gordon, Karin Olivas, and Amit Dar. 2004. "Impacts of Active Labor Market Programs: New Evidence from Evaluations with Particular Attention to Developing and Transition Countries." Social Protection Discussion Paper, No. 0402. Human Development Network, World Bank, Washington, DC.

Betts, Julian R. 1995. "Does School Quality Matter? Evidence from the National Longitudinal Survey of Youth." *The Review of Economics and Statistics* 77 (2): 231–50.

Blundell, R., L. Dearden, and B. Sianesi. 2005. "Evaluating the Effect of Education on Earnings: Models, Methods and Results from the National Child Development Survey." *Journal of Royal Statistical Society* Series A. 168 (3): 473–512.

Boissiere, M., J. B. Knight, and R. H. Sabot. 1985. "Earnings, Schooling, Ability, and Cognitive Skills." *American Economic Review* 75 (5): 1016–30.

Buchinsky, M. 1994. "Changes in the U.S. Wage Structure, 1963–1987: An Application of Quantile Regression." *Econometrica* 62: 405–58.

Card, David. 1995. "Using Geographic Variation in College Proximity to Estimate the Return to Schooling." In *Aspects of Labor Market Behavior: Essays in Honor of John Vanderkamp*, ed. Louis N. Christofides, E. Kenneth Grant, Robert Swidinsky, 201–22. Toronto, Buffalo and London: University of Toronto Press.

———. 1999. "The Causal Effect of Education on Earnings." In *Handbook of Labor Economics*, edition 1, volume 3, ed. O. Ashenfelter and D. Card, 1801–63. Amsterdam: North Holland.

———. 2001. "Estimating the Return to Schooling: Progress on Some Persistent Econometric Problems." *Econometrica* 69 (5): 1127–60.

Card, David E., and Alan B. Krueger. 1992. "Does School Quality Matter? Returns to Education and the Characteristics of Public Schools in the United States." *The Journal of Political Economy* 100 (1): 1–40.

Case, Anne. 2001. "The Primacy of Education." Research Program in Development Studies, Princeton University, Princeton, NJ.

Case, Anne C., and Motohiro Yogo. 1999. "Does School Quality Matter? Returns to Education and the Characteristics of Schools in South Africa." Department of Economics, Princeton University, Princeton, NJ.

Cawley, J., J. J. Heckman, and E. Vytlacil. 1998. "Cognitive Ability and the Rising Return to Education." Working Paper Series No. 6388, National Bureau for Economic Research, Cambridge, MA.

Chandra, Amitabh. 2003. "Is the Convergence of the Racial Wage Gap Illusory?" NBER Working Paper No. 9476, National Bureau of Economic Research, Cambridge, MA.

Cruz-Castro, Laura, and Gavan P. P. Conlon. 2001. "Initial Training Policies and Transferability of Skill in Britain and Spain." CSIC Working Paper No. 01-03, Unidad de Politicas Comparadas.

Cunha, Flavio, and James J. Heckman. 2007. "The Technology of Skill Formation." *American Economic Review* 97 (2): 31–47.

Cunha, Flavio, James J. Heckman, L. Lochner, and Dimitriy V. Masterov. 2006. "Interpreting the Evidence on Life Cycle Skill Formation." In *Handbook of Education Economics*, ed. Eric Hanushek and F. Welch, 697–812. Amsterdam: Elsevier North Holland.

Currie, Janet, and Enrico Moretti. 2003. "Mother's Education and the Intergenerational Transmission of Human Capital: Evidence from College Openings." *Quarterly Journal of Economics* 118 (4): 1495–1532.

Dar, Amit, and P. Zafiris Tzannatos. 1999. "Active Labor Market Programs: A Review of the Evidence from Evaluations." Social Protection Discussion Paper No. 9901, World Bank, Washington, DC.

de Ferranti, David, William F. Maloney, Guillermo E. Perry, Indermit Gill, J. Luis Guasch, Carolina Sanchez-Paramo, and Norbert Schady. 2003. *Closing the Gap in Education and Technology*. Latin American and Caribbean Studies. Washington, DC: World Bank.

Di Gropello, E. ed. 2006. *Meeting the Challenges of Secondary Education in Latin America and East Asia: Improving Efficiency and Resource Mobilization*. Washington, DC: World Bank.

Diaz, J., H. Ñopo, J. Saavedra, and M. Torero. 2004. "Ethnicity and Access to Education in Urban Peru." Group of Analysis for Development (GRADE), Lima, Peru.

Duflo, Esther. 2001. "Schooling and Labor Market Consequences of School Construction in Indonesia: Evidence from an Unusual Policy Experiment." *American Economic Review* 91 (4): 795–813.

———. 2004. "The Medium Run Effects of Educational Expansion: Evidence from a Large School Construction Program in Indonesia." *Journal of Development Economics* 74 (1): 163–97.

Fields, Gary S. 2007. "Labor Market Policy in Developing Countries: A Selective Review of the Literature and the Needs for the Future." Policy Research Working Paper No. 4362, World Bank, Washington. DC.

Finnie, Ross, and Ronald Meng. 2001. "Cognitive Skills and the Youth Labor Market." *Applied Economics Letter* 8 (10): 675–9.

———. 2002. "Minorities, Cognitive Skills, and Incomes of Canadians." *Canadian Public Policy* 28: 257–73.

Flabbi, Luca, Stefano Paternostro, and Erwin R. Tiongson. 2007. "Returns to Education in the Economic Transition: A Systematic Assessment Using Comparable Data." Policy Research Working Paper No. 4225, World Bank, Washington, DC.

Girma, S., and A. Kedir. 2005. "Heterogeneity in Returns to Schooling: Econometric Evidence from Ethiopia." *Journal of Development Studies* 41 (8): 1405–16.

Glewwe, Paul 2002. "Schools and Skills in Developing Countries: Education Policies and Socioeconomic Outcomes." *Journal of Economic Literature* 40 (2): 436–82.

Green, D. A., and W. C. Riddell. 2001. "Literacy, Numeracy and Labor Market Outcomes." Discussion Paper 01-05, Department of Economics, University of British Columbia.

———. 2003. "Literacy and Earnings: An Investigation of the Interaction of Cognitive and Unobserved Skills in Earnings Generation." *Labor Economics* 10: 165–84.

Haan, Hans Christiaan, and Nicholas Serriere. 2002. "Training for Work in the Informal Sector: Fresh Evidence from West and Central Africa." International Training Center of the ILO, Turin, Italy.

Hahn, J., P. Todd, and W. Van der Klaauw. 2002. "Identification and Estimation of Treatment Effects with a Regression-Discontinuity Design." *Econometrica* 69 (1): 201–09.

Halaby, Charles N. 1994. "Overeducation and Skill Mismatch." *Sociology of Education* 67 (1): 47–59.

Hanushek, Eric A. 2005. "Alternative School Policies and the Benefits of General Cognitive Skills." *Economics of Education Review* 26: 447–62.

Hanushek, Eric. A., and Dennis D. Kimko. 2000. "Schooling, Labor-Force Quality, and the Growth of Nations." *The American Economic Review* 90 (5): 1184–208.

Hanushek, Eric A., and Ludger Woessmann. 2007. "The Role of Education Quality for Economic Growth." Policy Research Working Paper No. 4122, World Bank, Washington, DC.

Hawley, Joshua D. 2003. "Comparing the Payoff to Vocational and Academic Credentials in Thailand Over Time." *International Journal of Educational Development* 23: 607–25.

Heckman, James J. 1979. "Sample Selection Bias as a Specification Error." *Econometrica* 47 (1): 153–61.

———. 1995. "Lessons from the Bell Curve." *Journal of Political Economy* 103 (5): 1091–120.

Heckman, James J., Anne Layne-Farrar, and Petra Todd. 1995. "Does Measured School Quality Really Matter? An Examination of the Earnings-Quality Relationship." NBER Working Paper Series No. 5274, National Bureau of Economic Research, Cambridge, MA.

Heckman, James J., Lance J. Lochner, and Petra E. Todd. 2006. "Earnings Functions, Rates of Return and Treatment Effects: The Mincer Equation and Beyond." In *Handbook of the Economics of Education*, Volume 1, ed. E. R. Hanushek and F. Welch, chapter 7. North-Holland.

Hertz, Thomas. 2003. "Upward Bias in the Estimated Returns to Education: Evidence from South Africa." *American Economic Review* 93 (4): 1354–68.

Johanson, Richard K., and Arvil V. Adams. 2004. "Skills Development in Sub-Saharan Africa." World Bank Regional and Sectoral Studies, World Bank, Washington, DC.

Jolliffe, Dean. 1998. "Skills, Schooling, and Household Income in Ghana." *World Bank Economic Review* 12: 81–104.

Katz, Eliakim, and Oded Stark. 1987. "International Migration under Asymmetric Information." *Economic Journal* 97: 718–26.

Katz, Lawrence F., and Kevin M. Murphy. 1992. "Changes in Relative Wages, 1963–1987: Supply and Demand Factors." *Quarterly Journal of Economics* 107: 35–78.

King, E. M. 1997. "Who Pays for Education in Indonesia?" In *Marketizing Education and Health in Developing Countries: Miracle or Mirage?* ed. C. Colclough. New York: Oxford University Press.

Kingdon, G. 1998. "Does the Labour Market Explain Lower Female Schooling in India?" *Journal of Development Studies* 35 (1): 39–65.

Kingdon, G., and J. Knight. 2004. "Unemployment in South Africa: The Nature of the Beast." *World Development* 32 (3): 391–408.

Kingdon, Geeta, and Mans Soderbom. 2007a. "Education, Skills, and Labor Market Outcomes: Evidence from Ghana." Background paper prepared for the World Bank study, "Linking Education Policy to Labor Market Outcomes." Washington, DC. (Forthcoming in World Bank Education Working Paper Series)

———. 2007b. "Education, Skills, and Labor Market Outcomes: Evidence from Pakistan." Background paper prepared for the World Bank study, "Linking Education Policy to Labor Market Outcomes." Washington, DC. (Forthcoming in World Bank Education Working Paper Series)

Krueger, Alan B., and Mikael Lindahl. 2001. "Education for Growth: Why and for Whom?" *Journal of Economic Literature* 39 (4): 1101–36.

LaLonde, R. J. 1986. "Evaluating the Econometric Evaluations of Training Programs with Experimental Data." *American Economic Review* 76 (4): 604–20.

Lange, Fabian, and Robert Topel. 2006. "The Social Value of Education and Human Capital." In *Handbook of Education Economics*, ed. Eric Hanushek and F. Welch, 459–509. Amsterdam: Elsevier North Holland.

Laszlo, Sonia. 2005. "Self-Employment Earnings and Returns to Education in Rural Peru." *Journal of Development Studies* 41 (7): 1247–87.

Lee, David. 2005. "Training, Wages, and Sample Selection: Estimating Sharp Bounds on Treatment Effects." NBER Working Paper No. 11721, National Bureau of Economic Research, Cambridge, MA.

Lee, Lung-Fei. 1983. "Generalized Econometric Models with Selectivity." *Econometrica* 51 (2): 507–12.

Lukyanova, Anna, Yevgeniva Savchenko, Vladimir Gimpelson, Rostislav Kapelyushnikov, and Hong Tan. 2007. "Skills Shortages and Training in Russian Enterprises." Policy Research Working Paper No. 4222, World Bank, Washington, DC.

Machado, J., and J. Mata. 2000. "Box-Cox Quantile Regression and the Distribution of Firm Sizes." *Journal of Applied Econometrics* 15 (3): 253–74

Manacorda, Marco. 2007. "Issues in Estimating the Returns to Technical and Vocational Education." Background paper prepared for the World Bank study, "Linking Education Policy to Labor Market Outcomes." Washington, DC.

Manacorda, Marco, Carolina Sanchez-Paramo, and Norbert Schady. 2005. "Changes in Returns to Education in Latin America: The Role of Demand and Supply of Skills." CEP Discussion Paper No. 712, Center for Economic Policy, London School of Economics and Political Science, United Kingdom.

Martins, Pedro S., and Pedro T. Periera. 2004. "Does Education Reduce Wage Inequality? Quantile Regression Evidence from 16 Countries." *Labor Economics* 11 (3): 355–71.

McIntosh, Steven. 2004. "The Returns to Apprenticeship Training." CEP Discussion Paper No. 622, Center for Economic Policy, London School of Economics and Political Science and Political Science, United Kingdom.

McIntosh, Steven, and Anna Vignoles. 2001. "Measuring and Assessing the Impact of Basic Skills on Labor Market Outcomes." *Oxford Economic Papers* 53 (3): 453–81.

Min, Wei-Fang, and Mun Chiu Tsang. 1990. "Vocational Education and Productivity: A Case Study of the Beijing General Auto Industry Company." *Economics of Education Review* 9 (4): 351–64.

Mincer, J. 1974. *Schooling, Experience and Earnings*, New York: Columbia University Press.

Moll, Peter G. 1998. "Primary Schooling, Cognitive Skills, and Wages in South Africa." *Economica* 65 (258): 263–84.

Monk, Courtney, Justin Sandefur, and Francis Teal. 2007. "Apprenticeship in Ghana." Background Paper prepared jointly for the World Bank study "Linking Education Policy to Labor Market Outcomes" and Ghana Job Creation and Skills Development study. Available as Vol. II of Report No. 40328 – GH.

Moretti, Enrico. 2004a. "Estimating the Social Return to Higher Education: Evidence from Longitudinal and Repeated Cross-Sectional Data." *Journal of Econometrics* 121: 175–212.

———. 2004b. "Workers' Education, Spillovers and Productivity: Evidence from Plant-Level Production Functions." *American Economic Review* 94 (3): 656–90.

Murnane, Richard J., J. B. Willett, Y. Duhaldeborde, and J. H. Tyler. 2000. "How Important are the Cognitive Skills of Teenagers in Predicting Subsequent Earnings?" *Journal of Policy Analysis and Management* 19 (4): 547–68.

Murnane, Richard J., John B. Willett, and Frank Levy. 1995. "The Growing Importance of Cognitive Skills in Wage Determination." *The Review of Economics and Statistics* 77 (2): 251–66.

Mwabu, G., and T. P. Schultz. 1996. "Education Returns Across Quantiles of the Wage Function: Alternative Explanations for Returns to Education by Race in South Africa." *American Economic Review* 86: 335–9.

Neuman, Shoshana, and Adrian Ziderman. 2001. "Can Vocational Education Improve the Wages of Minorities and Disadvantaged Groups? The Case of Israel." IZA Discussion Paper No. 348, Institute for the Study of Labor, Bonn.

Nielsen, Chantal P. 2007. "Immigrant Overeducation: Evidence from Denmark." Policy Research Working Paper No. 4234, World Bank, Washington, DC.

OECD (Organisation for Economic Co-operation and Development). 2000. "A Comprehensive Framework for Indicators of the Transition from Initial Education to Working Life: Perspectives from the OECD Thematic Review." International Workshop on Comprehensive Data on Education-to-Work Transitions, Paris, June 21–23.

———. 2007. *PISA 2006 Science Competencies for Tomorrow's World*. Vol. I. Paris: Organisation for Economic Cooperation and Development.

O'Higgins, Niall. 2002. "Youth Employment in Asia and the Pacific: Analytical Framework and Policy Recommendations." Paper prepared for ILO/Japan Tripartite Regional Meeting on Youth Employment in Asia and the Pacific, Bangkok, Thailand, February 27–March 1.

O'Keefe, Philip, and Maitreyi B. Das. 2007. "Enterprises, Workers, and Skills in Urban Timor-Leste." Policy Research Working Paper No. 4177, World Bank, Washington, DC.

Olivetti, Claudia, and Barbara Petrongolo. 2005. "Unequal Pay or Unequal Employment? A Cross-Country Analysis of Gender Gaps." Unpublished, London School of Economics and Political Science.

Oreopoulos, Philip. 2006. "Average Treatment Effects of Education when Compulsory School Laws Really Matter." *American Economic Review* 96 (1): 152–75.

Patrinos, Harry, and C. Ridao-Cano. 2006. "Demand for Secondary Education in Latin America and East Asia." In *Meeting the Challenges of Secondary Education in Latin America and East Asia: Improving Efficiency and Resource Mobilization,* ed. E. di Gropello. Washington, DC: World Bank.

Patrinos, Harry, Cris Ridao-Cano, and C. Sakellariou. 2006. "Estimating the Returns to Education: Accounting for Heterogeneity in Ability." Policy Research Working Paper No. 4040, World Bank, Washington, DC.

Psacharopoulos, G. 1994. "Returns to Investment in Education: A Global Update." *World Development* 22 (9): 1325–43.

Psacharopoulos, George, and Harry A. Patrinos. 2004. "Returns to Investment in Education: A Further Update." *Education Economics* 12 (2): 111–34.

Psacharopoulos, George, and Eduardo Velez. 1992. "Schooling, Ability, and Earnings in Colombia, 1988." *Economic Development and Cultural Change* 40 (3): 629–43.

Revenga, Ana, Carlos Silva-Jaurequi, Lucia Haulikova, Thesia Garner, Anton Marcincin, Dena Ringold, Manuel de la Rocha, Carolina Sanchez-Paramo, Helen Shahriari, Diane Steele, Katherine Terrell, Ruslan Yemtsov, Iveta Radicova, and Michal Vasecka. 2002. *Slovak Republic: Living Standards, Employment and Labor Market Study.* Washington, DC: World Bank.

Riboud, Michelle, Yevgeniva Savchenko, and Hong Tan. 2007. "The Knowledge Economy and Education and Training in South Asia: A Mapping Exercise of Available Survey Data." Human Development Unit, South Asia Region, World Bank, Washington, DC.

Rutkowski, Jan. 2003. "Why is Unemployment so High in Bulgaria?" Policy Research Working Paper No. 3017, World Bank, Washington, DC.

Sandefur, Justin, Francis Teal, and Pieter Serneels. 2006. "African Poverty through the Lens of Labor Economics: Earnings and Mobility in Three Countries." Working Paper Series No. 060, Global Poverty Research Group, Economic and Social Research Council, United Kingdom.

Schultz, T. Paul. 2003. "Evidence of Returns to Schooling in Africa from Household Surveys: Monitoring and Restructuring the Market for Education." Economic Growth Center Discussion Paper No. 875, Yale University, New Haven, CT.

Staiger, Douglas, and James H. Stock. 1997. "Instrumental Variables Regression with Weak Instruments." *Econometrica* 65 (3): 557–86.

Teal, F. 2007. "Formal and Informal Employment in Ghana: Job Creation and Skills." Background paper prepared for the study on "Linking Education Policy to Labor Market Outcomes." World Bank, Washington, DC.

Teal, Francis, and Justin Sandefur. 2007. "Understanding the Informal and Formal Sector in Africa: A Note." Unpublished, Department of Economics, Oxford University, United Kingdom.

Teal, Francis, Justin Sandefur, and Courtney Monk. 2007. "Apprenticeship in Ghana." Background Paper prepared jointly for the World Bank study "Linking Education Policy to Labor Market Outcomes" and Ghana Job Creation and Skills Development study. Available as Vol. II of Report No. 40328-GH, World Bank, Washington, DC.

Van der Velden, Rolf K. W., and Maarten H. J. Wolbers. 2007. "How Much Does Education Matter and Why? The Effects of Education on Socio-economic Outcomes among School-leavers in the Netherlands." European Sociological Review 23 (1): 65–80.

World Bank. 2006. *World Development Report 2007: Development and the Next Generation.* Washington, DC: World Bank.

———. 2007. "Mongolia: Building the Skills for the New Economy."

Index